The Wealthy Teen

A Guide for Teens, Parents and Mentors

By Lorna Hegarty and Carly

ISBN: 978-0-9698936-8-4

Published by: LCH Resources Limited
                 www.LCHResources.com

First Printing October 2006
Second Edition – May 2010
Third Edition – March 2016

This book is designed to provide accurate and authoritative information on the subject of personal finances from the viewpoint of both mentor and teen. While all the stories and anecdotes described are based on true experiences, most of the names are pseudonyms and some situations have been changed slightly for educational purposes and to protect individual privacy. This book is sold with the understanding that neither the Author nor the Publisher is engaged in rendering legal/accounting or other professional services by publishing this book. As each situation is unique, questions relevant to personal finances and specific to the individual should be addressed to an appropriate professional to ensure that the situation has been evaluated carefully and properly. The Author and Publisher specifically disclaim any liability, loss, or risk that is incurred as a consequence, directly or indirectly, of the use and application of any of the contents of this work.

CONTENTS

FOREWARD

It goes without saying that each one of us wants a bright future for our children. No matter where we began or what our circumstances were, we do our best in every way to improve on the model we grew up with, in order to make a better life for our daughters and our sons. The only thing that prevents us from achieving our goal is a scarcity of knowledge (information is everywhere, but not necessarily accurate or actionable) and a lack of workable tools.

As each of my own children came to recognize and understand the principle of cause and effect, I began to teach them the basics of money management along with the other life skills I believed were essential to them. In much the same way that I clarified the need for personal hygiene and a balanced diet – showing them what happens when you <u>don't</u> follow a few basic rules – I also gave them practical examples that illustrated the outcome when money was squandered and when it was put to work.

To enable them to succeed and fail in a protected environment – in other words, to allow them to make mistakes without having to pay too great a price – I designed a mentoring program in which we acted as teams rather than as parent and child.

- I was there when <u>they</u> needed me, not when I thought it was best for them.

- I designed tangible goals they could appreciate; I devised simple exercises that would make sense to them.
- We set down schedules that allowed all of us to organize our time for maximum quality and minimum waste.
- We created a forum in which we could air out our differences without fear of punishment, where we could applaud each other's success.

As time passed, my children began to exhibit a quality of personal empowerment that was not shared by their peers. Friends and neighbors commented with increasing frequency that my children and I enjoyed close relationships as compared to the sometimes indifferent and sullen resentment that seemed to be the norm.

When I spoke about these unexpected outcomes with other parents, they were unanimous in their recommendation that I put together a book that detailed my steps so that others might duplicate my results.

I went home and discussed the idea with my children. My sons gave it a 100% thumbs up and my fifteen-year-old daughter, Carly (today, with this 3rd Edition, she is 24), wanted to help write the book.

The Wealthy Teen is the result. It is a collaborative effort that brings together two very different perspectives: those of both the parent and the teen, working as a team. It provides a template that will help you build a strong mentoring association with your children as you empower them to achieve success. It presents practical tips and do-able techniques that you can use every day – starting now! – to build a rewarding relationship and a brighter future for the people you love.

SUGGESTIONS ON HOW TO USE THIS BOOK:

As a parent, care provider, relative, mentor, or someone who wants to assist a young person navigate the world of money, you may wish to read this book first on your own and do the exercises. Having completed the exercises, you can then work with your teen (or young person) to have them go through the exercises and share your findings, and build some plans for going forward. You could both have a copy of the book, and set aside time to review the exercises when you have had time to complete them.

As a teen, you can read this book on your own, do the exercises, and discuss with someone you respect that has good money sense. You could also get a group of like-minded friends together to discuss.

***

Here is what 15-year-old Carly wrote for the 1st Edition:

Hey, my Mom's totally right!

Hi everyone, this is Carly. My Mom has been working with me on managing my money for like, forever. When I was just starting school, she sat me down with my brothers. I was seven years old back then; Dru was seventeen and Matt was just about to turn fifteen – the same age I am now. They had all these piggy banks crammed full of money and my Mom said, "Carly, it's time we got you started too."

We had these weekly family meetings where they were always talking about their goals and I wanted to be talking about my goals too. When my Mom made the announcement, the next thing that happened was totally cool: Dru and Matt each gave me five whole dollars in coins, saying, "Go for it, Carly! You can do it too."

Yeah, I know: you're thinking $10 is no big deal, but way back when I was seven, it was a major thing. Imagine your brother handing over a bunch of money to you, just because he wants you to succeed in life. Like I said, it's a major thing.

Then they showed me how to divide my money – just like we're going to show you in the pages to come – so that it did the most good, and they told me that making money work for you was cool. That was how I got started and since then, even though I've had some tough decisions to make, it's been lots of fun!

What I'm trying to say is that this isn't one of those books where everything is boring and 'good for you'. This is a book that can help you get the things you want without making you crazy along the way.

All I'm asking you to do is give it a chance and let us know how it ends up working for you.

My Mom made it easy and fun for us to learn how to put our money to work and I know we can help you too!

See you later. Don't forget to check out my Diary at the back of the book.

Bye for now!

***

2016 Update from Carly –

My money management skills have stayed with me over the last 10 years. I continue to deposit money into my RRSP account, have a savings account, and I hold a trading account for stocks and mutual funds. I enjoy researching the market.

I have followed my dream of being a photographer and earning my income this way. I had a plan, and I worked in a few photo studios, and at the CN Tower in Toronto in the photography department. This opened the door for me to get a job working on a cruise ship as a photographer. I was able to see many wonderful places all over the world, and I caught the travel bug.

I set a new goal for myself – to work and live in Australia within a year of leaving the cruise ship position. I took a retail job so that I could save for a plane ticket, work visa and money required to enter Australia.

A year later, I have worked as a photographer at a Koala Sanctuary, and on a lovely resort island in Australia. My new plan is to go to school in Australia and do photo shoots on the side to earn money as I learn.

I can't tell you how many people told me that I would never earn a living as a photographer, even the guidance counselor at my high school! With the encouragement of my mom, dad, and brothers, I am doing what I love, earning a living as a photographer.

I have continued with the practices of the Wealthy Teen, and assigned my money to separate accounts so I can keep track of it. I am a good saver, and really watch any purchases I make. I have no debt, and pay my credit card in full monthly.

I still follow the suggestions in this book, as they are timeless. You might want to as well!

Back to Lorna

Before I became a Mom, as Carly calls me, I had a full-time career as a Human Resources professional. While the children were young, I shifted my focus to devote my time and energy to my family. The children have long since been able to manage the everyday details of living without my close supervision, and I have shifted my focus back to HR management, this time as a Life and Business Coach.

Throughout these changes, I have always seen my primary function as that of a catalyst: someone who enables others to reach beyond their potential and achieve success. To be effective in this role, I have had to recognize and apply two very important truths:

> The first truth is aptly phrased in that wonderful remark by Beatle's legend, John Lennon: "Life is what happens while you're busy making other plans."

I'm going to paraphrase it for our use here as follows: Unless you take the time NOW to organize a life strategy that you can implement, a little bit every day as time goes by, the goals you seek for yourself and your children will forever remain out of reach.

> The second truth is that no two people are exactly alike. What I mean by this is that we are all individuals with our own thoughts and realities, and ideas that work for me may not work as well for you.

That is why Carly and I have created a template with lots of flexibility: so that you and your children can approach this exciting challenge in ways that are best suited for all of you.

Each teen I have raised has worked with the energy of money in different ways as they grew. Matthew liked to spend and learned to save; Dru liked to put money away and now he looks forward to the occasional reward. Carly was and is, a combination of the two.

As their mentor, I have seen myself change with the passing years too: becoming better equipped to share my knowledge and my own money sense to help them grasp the value of fiscal responsibility.

You are changing as well. The priorities you set for yourself before your children were born, have been replaced by other, more pressing realities. Your days are hectic, your focus is split in a million different directions and there simply aren't enough hours in the day. Though you care deeply about your children and want them to have a better life, you wonder how on earth you're supposed to find the time to even read this book, let alone implement the strategies Carly and I have devised.

Because I've been there too, I know how frazzled you can feel when someone tells you that you need to add one more burden to your overwhelming load. I've gone to great lengths to make this material easy to absorb and even easier to apply.

- Each simple step provides the basis for the step that follows.
- Each short-term goal is designed to empower your children to get involved in the process more and more, so that you do less and less of the hands-on work yourself.

As they acquire a greater sense of ownership of their success, your children will let down their defenses and welcome your support. The lines of communication will open as they never have before.

These statements are not empty promises. They are proven truths. Respect – for yourself and for others – is the vehicle you are learning to operate as a team. Happiness and prosperity are the destinations this vehicle will help you reach.

There is a third truth I want to share with you before we get on with the book: Everyone makes mistakes. I made lots of them and you will, too. The point is that no matter what happens as a result of your efforts, whether you see it as a success or a failure right now, it is a valuable lesson learned.

Success does not come without a price. Whether you have a little money or a lot, whether you succeed every time or have more than your share of failures, you must be willing to keep at it if you want to reap the rewards, and see your children become successful in their own lives.

True wealth is much more than an accumulation of dollars and cents. To be truly wealthy you must respect all the gifts you have: good health and happiness, great relationships and worthy goals. You must respect yourself as an individual and acknowledge your flaws. You must respect your unique accomplishments and honor your dreams and goals.

Our Purpose

The purpose of this book is to enable you to mentor your children and inspire them to handle themselves and their money with maturity and integrity.

Money plays such a complicated role in our lives. There are so many reasons people spend money, beyond paying the rent and putting food on the table. For some people, spending makes them feel good about themselves. When spending feeds a need that is not properly addressed, it can take over their lives, putting them in debt and making everyone around them unhappy.

If your children are like most teens, even as they try to follow your lead they will be fighting the pressures their friends place on them to follow the latest trends. They will be tempted to cave in to peer pressures and join them, and you will need to fight the temptation to step in.

Our role in this delicate process is to give you the tools that will empower them to

- trust their instincts
- make choices that work best for them

They are also designed to teach you how to let go.

The transformation won't happen overnight, but it will come in time as you follow the steps and everyone on the team has the opportunity to learn and grow.

The Wealthy Teen identifies the broadest definition of wealth and clarifies the vast difference between *being* rich and merely having and spending money. It provides exercises that help you take control of the ways you reward and respect yourself. It empowers you to take control of your life.

What is a Mentor?

A 'mentor' is a person who guides and advises you in the choices you make and the actions you take. More than a teacher, a mentor is also a friend: someone who will listen and be there when you're in need of someone who understands. A mentor can be anyone who has the time and the know-how to help someone they love.

This said, you, the parent, may have a mentor – just as you, the teen, can have a mentor. In this process of learning about wealth, the parent can naturally be a mentor to his/her child.

It's All About YOU

Our goal is to start a mentoring movement. Carly and I want you to be so successful, so completely in control of your life that we can point to you and say to others who follow... "Mentoring teams of parents and teens can change the world!"

It's true. You CAN change the world. All you need are the tools, a few practical tips and a little training.

Consider this truth: If where you are *today* is a result of thoughts and actions taken in the *past*, then where you want to be *tomorrow* will be determined by the thoughts and actions you take *today*. Carly and I are here to help you reach that goal.

What You Will Find Inside

- Where do our ideas and attitudes about money come from?

- How much of this do we pass on to our family, or pick up from our friends?
- What dictates how much we can earn and how much we can save?
- Can we earn more? Can we save more?

This book will help you discover the answers to these questions and more. It will help you learn what makes you think and act the way you do on the subject of wealth. It will help you learn how to manage your money and teach you what to do to feel comfortable making money decisions.

The Wealthy Teen is divided into 5 parts:

- Part One, "*Where Our Beliefs Begin*", prepares you and your teen for the work to come and helps you define your ⓔ Potential.
- Part Two, "*The Universal Laws*", identifies the Universal Laws that govern our lives.
- Part Three, "*Applying the Wisdom*", provides the tools to build a great financial future.
- Part Four, "*Building Your Money Baskets*", deals with money management and sets you on the life-long path to greater success.
- Part Five, "*Entrepreneurship and Your ⓔ Potential*", provides a questionnaire that allows you to determine your ⓔ Potential. These insightful

questions will reveal the qualities you already have, and the qualities you can learn, to create wealth through successful money management.

* * *

And more from 15-year-old Carly:

*Yeah! And Part Six of the book is "Carly's Diary"! I can hardly wait till you see it. You'll find out how to set up your piggy banks, how to psyche yourself **into** saving and **out of** spending on stuff that's nothing more than the Crave of the Day. And you'll get to hear all about this cool idea I had to make money!*

Lorna (and 25-year-old Carly!)

P.S. I'll be writing (mostly) for the parent or the teen mentor – but don't get distracted by that if you are a teen reader! It is ALL for you!

PART ONE:

Where Our Beliefs Begin

How You've Been Hard-Wired about Wealth

Consider this: Now as a parent of teens, look back on how financially beneficial it would have been if someone had taught you more about money. If someone had said to you as a teen earning your first money, "Buy that house right now – you are of age – do it immediately! Because securing a home for yourself will never be cheaper." ... Would you have listened?

It is the rare teen who goes into business (though more and more are doing so; it has become easier and more acceptable than it was for us), or who purchases something as major as real estate – and who does it because they have a *plan*.

As children, most of us were given mixed signals about wealth. I mean that some of what we heard was outright negative or pessimistic, some of what we heard about money was neutral, and a share of what we heard was quite positive.

Though money was something everyone worked hard to get, it was never recognized or applauded as an end in itself. Having money in abundance – more than your 'fair share', whatever that meant – was considered to be selfish and innately wrong.

With phrases like 'stinking rich' and 'money is the root of all evil' and 'you can't buy happiness' placing a decidedly negative slant on wealth, it isn't hard to understand why we might grow up to see great wealth as an inappropriate goal to strive for. We grow up to believe that financial independence is almost impossible.

Focused on the traditional view that happiness comes from having a regular job and a steady paycheck and that a lifetime of work was the route to success, we diligently followed the teachings of those who had dedicated their lives to this belief. Just like them, we wound up feeling trapped, bored and broke.

What was wrong with this concept? It turns out that it was only *partly* true. Success is *partly* a result of holding a steady job, yes. But the other, critical part of the formula is *what we do with the money we earn*: how we manage it and make it work for us is what provides the foundation for our financial future and long-term success.

So it naturally follows that if our hard-wired notions of wealth and wealth management are fundamentally flawed, then the wisdom we have been sharing with our children is innately flawed as well.

What are your thoughts about money?

So what _are_ your thoughts about money? Is it a necessary evil, the root of all evil or the great facilitator? Do you want immeasurable wealth and are you willing to work actively toward that goal? Or do you prefer to live from paycheck to paycheck and "just let things happen" in your financial life?

As we've said, the thoughts and feelings you have about money have been shaped by the ideas and feelings your parents and guardians had before you. Even if you decided to rebel and go the opposite route, your behavior simply reflects their actions and attitudes in reverse. Where they may have spent lavishly, you might save; where they gave generously to charities you might hold back.

To discover the ideas and views you carry within you, take a pen and paper and write down at least five things about your life as it relates to money. Don't hesitate to write the first thing that pops in your head! Don't edit your responses before writing them, because you know what? There are no right or wrong answers!

Use the following categories:

<u>Sentences or statements</u> you heard your parents use about money when you were growing up:

1. ....
2. ....
3. ....
4. ....
5. ....

<u>Ideas</u> about money that you carry with you to this day:

1. ....
2. ....
3. ....
4. ....
5. ....

Specific incidents that related to money:

1. ....
....

2. ....
....

3. ....
....

4. ....
....

5. ....
....

Assumptions about money that you have absorbed and followed over the years:

1. ....
....

2. ....
....

3. ....
....

4. ....
....

5. ....
....

Were your first thoughts about money positive ... or negative?

Let's look at the first set of sentences you wrote down. What do they tell you about your earliest influences regarding money? Are they positive or negative? Are they sentences like, *'Money doesn't grow on Trees'* or more like *'Spend and God will Send'*?

How do your parents' beliefs shape the person you are today?

- Do you think the same way your parents do?
- Do you echo the sentences you heard as a child?
- Do you consciously make it a point never to speak like them?

Let's move on to the five ideas you have written about money. Think over the questions below and write your answers:

- Do you think money is easy to make – or hard to come by?

  ....

- If money had a voice, what would money 'say' *to* you?

  ....

- What does it say *about* you?

  ....

- How much of it do you have in the bank?

  ....

- Do you like spending money on yourself – or on others?

  ....

- Are you perpetually broke?

  ....

- How much is 'enough' money?

  ....

Go back and take a close look at the incidents you chose in the exercise above. Check your 'gut' reaction. Were they fun things to do? Do you have sad or guilty memories? Do you feel a complicated mix of emotions?

Rate your experiences here with 1 being the lowest and the most negative incident, and 10 the highest and most positive incident:

Negative   Positive
1   2   3   4   5   6   7   8   9   10

Incident 1: ___

Incident 2: ___

Incident 3: ___

Incident 4: ___

Incident 5: ___

Total: _____

What is your total score? What does it say about you?

0-35: Low. Negative thoughts surround your ideas about money.

35- 55: Middle. Negative ideas about money outweigh positive ideas.

55- 75: You like having money and are optimistic in nature. Feelings of negativity still bog you down, especially when you have spent more than you should have.

75-100: Congratulations! The fact that you scored so high and are still reading this book shows an inquiring mind hungry for information and new ideas. You are very positive and optimistic with great ⓔ *Power*. Your entrepreneurial mindset sees opportunities everywhere.

Ask yourself why these particular experiences stick in your mind and what they tell you about your inner workings and thoughts as they relate to money and being wealthy.

Last but not least, let's analyze the five assumptions you have written about money. In the space provided, write the first thing that comes to mind. Don't stop to analyze and think it through:

- What do you assume to be the truth about money?

  ....

- Do you believe that money always shows up when you need it?

  ....

- Are you always short of cash and believe you will never have enough money to be happy/comfortable?

  ....

Study your assumptions for a moment. We'll return to them toward the end of this book and see how your perceptions regarding money may have changed.

SUCCESS = Money AND You

The preceding exercises (if you actually engaged in the process and wrote your answers down) should have given you a fair idea of the kind of attitudes and perceptions that influence your thinking about wealth. To reframe your thinking from negative to positive, the first thing you have to do is recognize that money is one half of the Success Formula of life. It is only 50% of the equation! To be a success and truly enjoy your life, the ingredients you must have to create an unbeatable Success Formula are Money AND You. It is the collaborative effort that makes it work.

Stop a Minute and Think!

How did we come to understand the basics of money management?

- Did we learn the principles of net profit and loss selling lemonade by the glass on hot summer afternoons?
- Did we truly grasp what it means to budget and save while our weekly allowance burned holes in our pockets?
- Was our math teacher focused on teaching the rules that govern equations or were they more concerned about the number of apples Johnny has left and what time one train meets another en route to its destination?
- Were our parents too busy balancing their own books to paint the picture in clear, simple terms?

If we didn't learn that managing money is a system based on rules, what did we learn?

Like everything else that we copy without question, what we learned were half-baked ideas and misconceptions that really don't work in the real world. This mixed bag of misinformation formed our belief that wealth is a matter of luck. If we were on top of things one week and broke the next, instead of doing a little work to change our money habits, we'd do a lot of work to change our luck.

Therefore...

If it is true that our attitudes, assumptions and ideas about money are based on the lessons we learned as children and throughout our formative years...

It naturally follows that, unless we do something to change the hard-wired beliefs we learned, our children will learn nothing of practical value about wealth and money management that they can take with them into the future.

Are you ready and willing to change what you have believed all your life in order to have a life of success and abundance?

How much you want to change to help yourself and others is up to you. If all that matters to you is the status quo and the approval of your peers, then that is all you will ever have. On the other hand, if you want to reach for success – and with it, unlimited wealth and the freedom it brings – there's no stopping you!

Adjusting Your Thoughts as Mentors

The first step toward greater financial success is to recognize the importance of your thoughts and how they shape your actions. Now that you have given some thought to the questions we posed earlier and you have expressed your attitudes, ideas and assumptions about money, it's time to involve your closest friends and family in the process as well.

You want to ask them to answer a question about *you*. The question is this:

"What do *you* think about my attitude toward money?"

Try not to get defensive and upset if you hear something you don't like. Remember, you have asked for their opinion! It can be very interesting and quite revealing to find out how someone close to you sees, hears or perceives the way you interact with money.

I asked a client of mine to do this exercise with a few of her friends after she had completed the earlier Q&A process. As a way of illustrating the incredible insights this step can offer you, I am going to share the results she obtained and the valuable insights she gained.

Susan believed she had a great attitude about wealth. She knew she would like to have more savings and would like to be earning more money as well, and overall, she felt confident that her friends would have very positive things to say about her ability to manage her money. When the replies came in, she was completely unprepared.

These are some of the comments her friends shared:

- When Susan has money it's suddenly Christmas; the rest of the time it's bare bones survival.
- Susan can be very frugal for a long time and then she'll suddenly blow a couple of hundred dollars on a purse or something she really didn't seem to want all that badly.
- Susan starts so many new projects. With the vitamin company, she was all excited until her sales didn't go well. She gave up after the first month and switched to selling candles part time. What would happen if she really committed to something?
- She'd make a great ad agency manager, but when I tell her how talented I think she is, she says she doesn't want the headache or the extra work.
- She keeps saying next year she'll make it big.
- Susan has had 3 jobs since I have known her and has nothing in savings, or in a retirement fund. Every time she changes jobs, she cashes out her money and spends it.

Susan had imagined herself as someone who knew exactly where she was going and what she was doing when it came to money. This 'together' image was shattered when she read her friends' replies. After she had recovered from the shock and surprise, she realized that she had been blind to the deeply entrenched behaviors that were so counter-productive to her success.

Susan came face-to-face with the truth about herself for the first time. She realized that she was far from having a well-planned life. She recognized that the goals she had were bits of one plan here and another plan there, rather than a cohesive whole. She had no financial or professional plan for her future that provided a step-by-step path connecting where she was today and where she wanted to be six months, a year, five years, or 50 years from now.

While she had planned some things, she hadn't harnessed the power of her mind to focus on her goals. She was like a ship adrift on the sea without a rudder or a compass. The engine was running and she was going round and round in circles.

To help Susan use the information her friends had provided to make productive changes in her life, I worked through the answers with her, like this:

- *'When she has money it's suddenly Christmas, the rest of the time it's bare bones survival.'*

  I explained to Susan that, like most of us, she didn't budget properly. When she received a big check, she spent a tiny bit of it paying down her bills and then splurged on 'feel-good' items as a reward. The rest of the time, she merely existed.

  Susan told me she believed that money would always show up when things got desperate, but she never connected her need and desire for money with the timing and amount or that it appeared at all.

- *'Susan can be very frugal for a long time, and then she'll suddenly blow a couple of hundred dollars on a purse or something she really didn't seem to want all that badly.*

Susan told me she was conscious of the fact that she struggled to save and wanted to save, but like a fanatic whose rigid diet is impossible to follow for very long, she sometimes fell off the wagon in a big way. The sad thing was that the things she bought made her happy for such a short time.

- *'Susan starts so many new projects. With the vitamin company she was all excited until her sales didn't go well. She gave up after the first month and switched to selling candles part time. What would happen if she really committed to something?'*

Susan always wanted to earn just a little more. That's why she signed up to sell vitamins and candles, not because the career or the products themselves held any interest for her. She had a vision of an ideal future in which she would be 'comfortable', pay bills on time and travel abroad for holidays. Yet she never followed through, projecting actual dollar goals or drawing up a proper Plan of Action.

Each one of Susan's many ventures made small amounts of money within the first few months, but because none of them excited her on their own merits, she would invariably shut down the operation when the added work became more of a liability than an asset and she got impatient with the process, disappointed with the results and bored.

- *'She'd make a great ad agency manager, but when I tell her how talented I think she is she says she doesn't want the headache or the extra work.'*

Susan knew she was talented, but she hadn't taken the time to sit down and *quantify* her skills in *tangible* terms. The thought of taking on a responsibility like managing an agency was overwhelming. Since she had no idea <u>why</u> she succeeded at anything, she had no idea what would cause her to fail. What if everything she had achieved so far was a fluke? To take on such a big risk felt like a chance she just couldn't afford to take.

- *'She keeps saying next year she'll make it big.'*

Susan was procrastinating for any number of reasons, the most likely one being that if you don't try, you can't fail. Aren't we taking about *fear*? We fear failure but we also fear success!

- *'Susan has had 3 jobs since I have known her and has nothing in her retirement fund. Every time she changes jobs she cashes out her money and spends it.'*

People like Susan underestimate the amount needed to retire comfortably, especially if the government is unable to fulfill its promise to support us. But even before that type of calculation, Susan may not even know how much her current lifestyle costs her from month to month! Remember – she doesn't pay *off* her debts, she only pays them *down.* Carrying debt forward is the opposite of wealth-mentality.

Each of us is a little bit like Susan. Even when we think we have it all figured out, what we usually have are a number of half-formed ideas, not a winning strategy at all. All too often, we are ready to give up when the process takes too long or the work is too tough.

Now it's your turn

To discover whether you are as organized and motivated as you believe yourself to be, ask three friends for their honest opinion about the way you deal with money. If they feel a bit awkward, let them know how much this is going to help you – and that you will gladly return the favor when they're ready to take the challenge themselves. For this exercise to work, the feedback needs to be honest. Tell them you'll provide them with a self-addressed stamped envelope and have them mail it back, or if you both agree you can use email for this exercise. Ask them to take some time to think about their answer before they respond.

Once you have the responses, compare them with the vision *you had of yourself.* Don't be upset if their replies sound critical. Their feedback will provide valuable input that will help you improve your chances for long-term financial freedom and success. Once you have their input you can look for common threads and things that surprise you. Be sure to follow up and thank your friends.

Now that you have your feedback you can compare it with your own assessment. It will be much easier to plan where you are going once you have taken a long, hard look at where you've been!

For Mentors:

Here's what my 3 Friends had to say about Me

Friend 1:
- -
- -
- -

Friend 2:
- -
- -
- -

Friend 3:
- -
- -
- -

With the homework successfully completed on yourself, as a mentor, it's time to shift your focus a little and think about your teen(s).

What We Are Teaching Our Teens

When we take on the role of mentor and guide for our children, we teach them what we know to be true. That is all we have, right? But what if what we thought was true ... isn't? What if what we thought we knew ... was incomplete?

For those of us who are working with an incomplete or flawed success formula as outlined earlier, we may have shown our children the importance of being steady and safe earners, but we will have failed to guide our children in taking those all-important next steps to achieve long-term success.

This is not entirely our fault. Without the support of our teachers or a history as investors ourselves, we have been unable to share our knowledge and instill confidence in our children when it comes to the business of teaching them to invest in themselves.

To make matters worse, while we have remained rooted in the outmoded 'lifetime career' mindset, the world has changed. The new generation we are raising is experiencing a different world from the one we had at their age. What has (or might have) worked for us is totally "old-school" or out of date for them.

Long-term, single-job careers are the exception today rather than the norm. People no longer expect to hold one job in one career path over the course of their working life, but rather to have as many as 10 different careers before they retire. Attempting to force this outmoded ideal onto the current reality is like trying to wedge a square peg into a round hole: it creates nothing but confusion, frustration and futility.

The bottom line is this: If we continue to teach our children to depend on outmoded ideas as they strive to take control of their lives and their futures, we are giving them a blueprint for failure.

How can we turn it around?

- By taking the time to re-examine the hard-wiring that has shaped our beliefs about wealth.
- By investing our energies in adopting new attitudes about wealth management.
- By passing this new-found wisdom along to our teens.

If we had to struggle all our lives to make ends meet, does it make any sense to program our children to do the same?

Of course not. If we are having or have had, a hard time acquiring and controlling money, we owe it to our children to give them a better plan for success.

If we have been stuck all our lives with an income of $X, why would we set that as the limit our teenagers can never cross?

If we are stingy with our own money, does this teach our teens to be the same or does it send them into spending frenzies in revolt?

It's time we realized that the same behavioral or emotional *influences* that shaped our thinking and acting about money and wealth will shape our children as well. Just as we were influenced by the adults and events in our youth, our teens will have their habits influenced by their own childhood experiences with you as well.

If pre-conceived notions led us to believe that our ability to manage money was the best, the same will be true of our teens. Just as the input from our friends gives us a better perspective on the truth, the same will be true for them.

Ask your teen to invite three friends to give their opinions, just as your friends did for you. Keep in mind the fact that they may not be very open to the idea of sharing their innermost thoughts. Be patient!

For Teens:

Here's what my 3 Friends had to say about Me

Friend 1:

Friend 2:

Friend 3:

Rewiring your Teen's Thoughts

Now that you are aware of the gap between your thoughts and the reality of your actions as well as the gap that exists for your teen, you can appreciate how much more difficult it is for teenagers to be financially aware. All the more reason to teach them the principles and attitudes of good money management from an early age. In doing so, not only will you lay the foundation of success at a young age: you will ensure a financially abundant and debt-free future for them.

What does the child you are mentoring think and feel about money? To find out, repeat the exercises you completed for yourself on the preceding pages.

Use this opportunity as an information underline exchange. In all likelihood, you will discover that your teen has absorbed many of your ideas and opinions. That's why this book is designed to get you talking to each other and exchanging ideas. To be really successful, both of you need to analyze your thoughts and feelings about money and set the same objectives. Be ready to discuss the answers without criticizing. They will be sure to reveal a lot about you!

Five sentence or statements you heard your parents use about money when you were growing up:
1. ....
2. ....
3. ....
4. ....
5. ....

Five ideas about money that you carry with you to this day:

1. ....
2. ....
3. ....
4. ....
5. ....

Five specific incidents that related to money:

1. ....
   ....
2. ....
   ....
3. ....
   ....
4. ....
   ....
5. ....
   ....

Five <u>assumptions</u> about money that you have absorbed and followed over the years:

1. ....
   ....
2. ....
   ....
3. ....
   ....
4. ....
   ....
5. ....
   ....

Teens:
Were your first thoughts about money positive ... or negative?

Let's go back to the first set of sentences. What do they tell you about your earliest influences regarding money? What have you been hearing your role models, your teachers, your mentors and your friends say about money? Are they positive or negative?

How do these sentences and thoughts shape your thinking? Do you think the same way as your mentors? Do you find yourself saying the same things you heard when you were growing up? Or do you consciously make it a point *never* to speak like them?

Now let's move on to the five ideas you have written about money. Think over the questions below and write down your answers:

- Do you think money is easy to make or hard to come by? Do you just have to ask for it, or do you have to work for it?

- What does money "say" to you? ("Come on, let's .....")

- What does it say about you? ("You are ......")

- How much do you have in the bank? Do you have a bank account?

- Do you like spending money on yourself?

- Are you perpetually broke?

- How much is 'enough' money? (Name a figure ...)

Go back and take a close look at the incidents you chose. Check your 'gut' reaction. Were they fun things to do? Do you have sad or guilty memories? Do you feel a complicated mix of emotions?

Rate your experiences here with 1 being the lowest and the most negative incident and 10 the highest and most positive incident:

Negative   Positive
  1   2   3   4   5   6   7   8   9   10

Incident 1:

Incident 2:

Incident 3:

Incident 4:

Incident 5:

Total: _____

What is your total score? What does it say about you?

0-35: Low. Negative thoughts surround your ideas about money. You feel you don't have enough and never will. It's time to make a change in your thinking and move to a 'half-full' way of thinking.

35- 55: Negative ideas about money outweigh your positive ideas.

55- 75: You like having money and are optimistic in nature. When you have spent more than you should, you wonder if it was wise to do so and where the next dollar will come from.

75-100: Congratulations! You seem to be a born winner. A very positive and optimistic person with great ⓔ power. You probably have an entrepreneurial mind and see opportunities everywhere you look.

Add your own thoughts here about the kind of person you are and what you want to be. Be specific in terms of goals and changes you want to make.

A Thought for Mentors

Just as the exercises revealed your state of mind and assumptions about money, they will reveal your teens' (your mentee's) thoughts and ideas relating to money as well. What do they think about it? How do they feel about it? What do they assume to be true?

It is quite possible that on a few points, your teen may not have all the answers. This is a good thing, because it will let you work toward a better understanding of money and success together. It is also possible that their answers may be very different from yours. Work together to gain an understanding of where these thoughts and practices might be coming from.

Remember: Your teens have a right to their own thoughts and opinions. Chances are good that you could have an interesting conversation based on some of their answers. Don't be too quick to judge them or decide whether they are right or wrong – just LISTEN!

Let's pause for a moment to look at what ⓔ Potential really is. Then we will move on to consider how to develop it.

Defining Your ⓔ Potential

ⓔ POTENTIAL? It is your *Earning* and *Entrepreneurial* capability.

ⓔ POTENTIAL is the potential that exists in each and every one of us to become more knowledgeable and smarter about our money and learn the many ways it can be *earned* and *managed* to accumulate wealth.

ⓔ POTENTIAL is the potential to be a smart risk-taker whose carefully calculated risks pay off.

In this book we do, it's true, focus on your potential for great earnings, but you know what? Earning is in direct correlation with other ⓔs as well:

> *Excellence* (in all we do), *Education* (about money, what you do to learn about any topic that excites you and to develop skills, knowledge and talents that help us *Earn*), and our *Enterprising Energy* (that inner *Enthusiasm* and *Excitement* we bring to our *Endeavors*) – they each contribute to your wealth!

Excellence: Anyone can do any easy or hard job halfway. You can "sort of" finish your homework. You can "sort of" listen to your best friend complain or happily tell you something. You can "sort of" understand what the boss or the teacher meant. *Anyone* can do that, but from now on, you need to remind yourself:

> I am *not* just anyone! Mediocrity is no longer an option for my actions, my thinking or my behaviors!

Anyone can work at a job. All you have to do is show up every day and take your paycheck home every two weeks, right? But people like you who realize your ⓔ *Potential* can have *careers and professions,* not just jobs. You do all your work – whatever it may be – with excellence. Find the beauty in the work. Imagine who will be looking at it afterwards ... with awe and respect at a job superlatively done.

How do you achieve that? You learn.

Education: They say the best public speakers or presenters know 40 times more about their subject than they can share in any speech. Can you say that you know 40 times more about your work than anyone else? You should aim for that level of knowledge, and see how it will help you perform it with excellence.

Anyone can go to school, grab the diploma and never open a book or go to a lecture or class again. That is what mediocre people do. There are millions of those people out there!

You, however? You never stop learning. That need not cost you a penny – not with the internet, public libraries and television! We know a lot of Do-It-Yourself individuals whose first stop to learn how to do something new is the internet and YouTube videos. It is quick and easy to keep on learning. Even the great universities are now posting whole classes on the web with free access. You can learn anything you like without going back to school in a formal way. You just have to be open to doing it.

The best people and the best companies believe in continuous training (that is, *Education*) for themselves. They stay on the cutting edge that way. That's what Canadian-born Céline Dion did to advance her career: As an older teen, she learned English to expand her potential fan-base to the English-speaking listeners. Now hasn't that been successful for her??

Now you say about yourself:

I learn! What do I need to learn about or learn to do to improve my most loved hobby, skills or talents? What do I need to learn to make myself more valuable to my boss or my customers?

Earning: In this day and age, even teenagers (with parental blessings) are earning far more money than their own parents or grandparents at the same age. We will be looking in great detail at the various ways to do that in later pages and chapters, along with how to manage the money you earn.

Enterprising Energy, inner **Enthusiasm** and **Excitement**: We know a lot of teens who have a full high school or college study load and still somehow manage to work 25-35 hours a week at a paying job. That is what we call Energy! As older adults, we wind down the number of hours we can give inner and physical energy to. That does not excuse us from needing to bring our inner passion, Enthusiasm and Excitement to what we are doing. It is that inner fire that may come from our purpose in life, or why we do anything. The inner fire comes from a true passion for our life and what we do in our waking hours.

Say about yourself:

I do what I love. I love what I do.
It earns me my living, so I continue to invest in myself, my talents in this area, and my future as a wealthy individual.

I strive for and achieve Excellence in all my Endeavors.

You can invest in your future and in yourself through that career choice that comes from enthusiasm and excitement for it.

All of these are what we are calling your Ⓔ *Potential.*

Potential?

By developing our Ⓔ *Potential,* we develop our entrepreneurial and earning abilities and apply those abilities to every facet of our lives. In order to know which skills to develop to become truly successful, we need to understand our strengths and our weaknesses and the influence each of them have on our natural Ⓔ *Potential.*

This book will help you realize how much Ⓔ *Potential* you have.

<u>NOTE</u>: As a parent, it will perhaps open your eyes about how much potential your teen has as well – in all kinds of areas you did not consider "serious" before. Don't get stuck thinking that a young child's passion cannot create wealth for him. Look out into the world, and you readily see males and females making a good living (or better!) from something you today might be calling "frivolous" or a "waste of time."

> **Example:** As a youngster just able to walk, Suz loved to wander her parents' garden and yard, lie down and talk to the plants. Her parents thought they were raising a dreamer. Not so! Or at least, not entirely!

She got to know the Latin names of every one of those plants – by age 6. She started to earn pocket money by her youngest teens by creating herbal remedies for families of friends and neighbors, as well as doing a bit of garden improvements for them. Today, as an older teen, she studies herbology and botany at college, and is FAR ahead of her peers in knowledge and skill in these areas.

NOTE: As a teen (or, let's face it, as a parent), open your own eyes about a hobby or an interest you have that may seem to you, too, to have no hope of earning your living later in life, or even being mainstream in your own eyes. Why do you think so? Scan the internet and try to find people actually doing what you wish to do – they are out there! It is a huge world, and you have something to bring to it. You have great, great potential!

Example: As a young boy, Mark loved to knit and even use patterns to sew up his own cowboy-style shirts in all kinds of fabrics. He wore his creations, which – truth be told – were professional-grade! His parents didn't think that was an appropriate preoccupation for a boy. Hmmm. Not until he started at a famous Design School instead of college – on a full scholarship he had earned. Not until he won award after award from the business world for his original designs. Not until he started earning more money in a year than his parents earned in 5 years. Now his parents *get* that most of the visibly successful individuals in Mark's industry had traditionally been ... males! And were now fighting to stay visible in face of female competition.

Know yourself. Pursue your own talents, not those someone wishes you would or could develop. Accept your unique skills, talents, knowledge and passions. You have them inside you for a reason – and that reason is To Fulfill Your Potential.

Knowing how to shape your ⓔ *Potential* will help you achieve success.

Do you have a higher ⓔ *Potential* than you think? Does your teen? Can you earn more? Are you an average risk taker? Do you have the entrepreneurship abilities that can virtually spin money out of the air? Is your teen an entrepreneur in the making? Does your teen see an advantage to real property or other types of investment and ownership to create wealth for him or herself? No matter where you stand, there is room to learn and improve your ⓔ *Potential!*

As mentors and parents, we want our teens to earn a good living when they grow up. If our sons or daughters come to us and say they want to be musicians or painters or fashion designers, we may try to steer them into safer channels. Not because they don't have talent, but because we worry about the difficulties earning enough money that come with such esoteric pursuits. And yet, the reality is that almost every line of work has the potential to pay well if there is a commitment to developing the skills associated with it and to succeed.

Whether our children choose to read the Tarot cards or do glass blowing, or practice more conventional pursuits, it is only by examining their inherent ⓔ *Potential* and encouraging them to enhance their entrepreneurial attributes that they can expect to become wealthy and successful.

Where do you stand?

What is your personal definition of financial success? Do you want $40,000? How about $60,000 or $80,000? Why not reach for $100,000 or $200,000? Why stop there? Why not picture yourself earning $500,000? Who is stopping you from earning that kind of money?

You are!

Just as people strive to live within their comfort zones, they unconsciously limit themselves to income levels that match the mental image they have set for themselves. Because that mental image is firmly fixed in their minds, people come to believe that this is the way things were meant to be. To change the status quo, your mental image must undergo a radical transformation as well.

The words you have written about money and the way it makes you feel are an expression of the person you believe yourself to be. When you compare your actual earnings to your words, you'll find them to be a perfect match.

And that may or may not be what you want for yourself...

Attitude is a powerful thing. If some part of you disapproves of wealth, it doesn't make sense that you would have a positive attitude about acquiring money. If you did manage to earn vast sums, you'd get rid of it – or lose it somehow – just as quickly as it came. At the end of the day, you would find yourself left with as much money as you felt you truly deserved.

By the same logic, if your heart tells you that you are ready to take on the challenge that wealth carries with it, and your mind is willing to embrace the change, the money will begin to flow toward you rather than drift away. The existentialist philosophy holds true – You think, therefore you are.

Change cannot happen unless you welcome it. You need to listen to your heart as you ask yourself: "Do I deserve wealth? Can I step outside my comfort zone of safety and embrace success?"

Write down your working monthly income and today's date in the spaces provided and we'll come back to it later.

Working Income: .... Today's Date: ....

How much do you want to earn?

Let me repeat the question that was asked before: "Do you
want to earn more money, or are you happy with what you
are earning now?"

"*What a silly question,*" you are probably thinking.
"*Everyone wants to earn lots of money. Why wouldn't I?*"

While people will say they want to earn, save and invest
money, many of them <u>subconsciously</u> feel otherwise. There
are many factors that can prevent people from genuinely
desiring a lot of money. Their reasons can be as diverse as:

- Who, me? I don't *deserve* wealth!
- I don't come from money, so it'll never happen
- Money is the root of evil. All money is bad.
- It's immoral to be money-minded
- Money isn't the important thing in life
- It's good to be comfortable
- You have to be born wealthy to be rich
- Success stories happen in fairy tales
- You have to work really hard to be wealthy
- I'd have to deal with accountants, lawyers, etc.
- I just want to 'enjoy' life and not 'worry' about money
- It's your destiny to be poor or just self-sufficient; there's
  nothing you can do about it

> Add your own factors that genuinely prevent you from wanting and earning a lot of money. Be honest.
>
> _____
>
> _____

Did you recognize personal characteristics or feelings in any of the above statements? How about the one about 'being comfortable', or 'I don't deserve money' or the one about 'destiny'?

✓ Place a check mark beside any thoughts that may be familiar to you, and add to the list if you have more thoughts that may not have been noted.

Somehow, the universe seems to deliver both what we want and what we don't want. The problem is that we don't ask for enough of what we want. Or if we ask, we don't ask consistently for one thing. If we constantly think about what we don't want, somehow we attract that as well.

Is This You?

One day you decide to do something for your future, like invest your money. Things are exciting for a couple of days, but then it gets complicated and confusing and you put it on the back burner and move on to something else. On Monday, you want to be wealthy but by Thursday, you've gotten side-tracked with plans for the weekend when you can eat out, buy more stuff and put your feet up and relax. Sitting around with your friends, the talk turns to investments and first thing on Monday, the process starts all over again.

Or are you among those who set their eyes on something, aim for it and then set off with your laser sights set on the goal?

As a quick exercise, write down in the space provided what you would like to earn over a given period of time.

'I want to earn $_____/month by _____ [date]

What Is Your Income ⒺPotential?

So how much did you write down? How does that compare with the amount you are earning right now? If you are currently earning $30,000 did you write $40,000 or $45,000? Or did you write $100,000? How about a lot more?

You're probably thinking, "How am I supposed to achieve this figure? What can/must I do in order to earn this much?"

Every day, all around you, people become fed up with being fed up and something inside of them clicks. They decide to change jobs, or take on extra part-time work, to reach their dreams. They may start small businesses... selling solar cookers, making mobile apps, designing clothing, etc. They may decide to write books on things they are completely passionate about – Eradicating Hunger, Creating World Peace, How to ___, etc.

Why do they do this? The obvious answer is to make more money or to realize their dreams. But the real reason people take on new challenges is to change the mental image they've set for themselves *because the image they had doesn't work for them anymore.* If the person they see inside is focused on success, it stands to reason that success will enter their lives.

However, it takes more than wishing to make dreams come true. People may change their behaviors, but they need to change their attitudes too. Left to its own devices, your attitude will ruin all your hard work. You may tell yourself that you want different results, but those changes will never come if your belief system stays the same.

Let me repeat this, because it is key to turning things around from "too little" to "plenty":

Changes will never come if your belief system stays the same.

You get what you think. You create out there in the world what you believe inside yourself.

If you hold on to those beliefs picked up as a child from a modest family which had no faith in its ability to build wealth – those beliefs will be what blocks your wealth-building (or your success in any endeavor).

You may tell yourself that you want wealth, but if your attitude remains fixed on modest goals, or that you really don't deserve to be a wealthy person, you will find that you earn exactly as much money as it takes to reach those goals... because that's what you believe you deserve.

If this sounds a little too far-fetched to be taken seriously, it doesn't change the fact that it is true. Research has proven that when people set their limits at a certain level, they achieve that level easily but seldom rise above it to achieve more. When they learn to raise their own inner limits and change their attitude about success, their earnings quickly rose beyond those limits and kept rising every year.

When you realize what you're really capable of and what you are willing to do, the sky is the limit. Shoot for the moon and you're bound to hit a star. In the chapters that follow, you and your teen will learn and apply the same principles to your life to earn more.

What Is Your Teen's Income ⓔ Potential?

If your 13-year old teen were to come up to you and say, *'Hi Mom! I am going to earn $20,000 dollars this year, working part time. I have 5 free hours per week, so that should be plenty'*, how would you react? If you took it as foolish notion, you would teach your teen not to expect much from themselves or the universe.

Yet that scenario is very real.

Example:

> When he was just barely out of his teens, Sabeer Bhatia set up a partnership business and created Hotmail.com. One year later, they sold it for $400 million to Microsoft! And at this writing, Hotmail is still going strong. Sabeer knew exactly what he

wanted to earn and he made a commitment with his partner that they would sell when the asking price of $400 million was met.

Ideas like Hotmail don't come along every day, but it doesn't help you set goals to tell yourself this! However, to start with a more comfortable goal, you may want to set your sights on target that is a nice, but not impossible, stretch. Once you achieve it, start expanding your expectations with a new "stretch" goal.

Your teen could well be a millionaire in the making with the right training and tools. Take my daughter, Carly, for example. At the age of just 15, she already had over $1,500 dollars in her various savings accounts (and that sum has continued to grow) – and she hadn't started "working" yet. She had babysitting jobs, dog walking jobs, helping neighbors with gardening, and saved all her gift money.

Is she a millionaire in the making? You can bet she is! The credit goes to those who taught her to "think wealthy", and to her as well for stretching the boundaries of her mind and opening her vision to the possibilities in the world!

Compare this attitude with the 'entitlement' teen that has been taught to believe it is his right to ask for and be given money. What do you think will happen when this young man or woman discovers that the world isn't as giving as Mommy/Daddy/Aunty/Uncle? What kind of resources will they fall back on then?

How much your teens will earn starts with you. Will they follow your patterns of thinking? Will they do better than the people around them? A lot depends on what you teach them today. By setting a good example, by being positive and in control of your finances, you are already moving in the right direction.

Use the ideas that follow as a system to lay the foundations of financial success in your lives. You may already be partway there and just need a few reminders to help you out, or you may need some guidance to help yourself before you help your teen.

The two of you should read this book together as a team so that you can learn and apply its principles to achieve your goals. Copy and post the next page where both of you can see it every day.

Make a collage with pictures that recreate your goals and put it up on a wall. Visually, mentally and personally reaffirm your goals every day.

My Goal List

- My favorite "fun" goal is

- My top "stretch" goal is

- My top 3-month goal is

- My top one-year goal is

- My big, multi-year goal is

- My biggest goal and heart's desire is

Completion Date

- My favorite "fun" goal

- My top "stretch" goal

- My top 3-month goal

- My top one-year goal

- My big, multi-year goal

- My biggest goal and heart's desire
    -

Reaching for the Stars

Now that both of you have gone through our introductory exercises, you may see _the need to review and change your money mindset_.

Every time you find yourself thinking something negative, the steps we provide on the pages that follow can teach you to refocus your thoughts to your very positive your goal for success (or wealth or ___) for yourself and your family.

You have to desire success whole-heartedly. You have to commit to it and do whatever it takes to be successful.

Be Visual

- If you want to focus on one particular goal, write the goal down on a piece of paper.
- Draw a picture of it or find it in a magazine and cut it out to put on that piece of paper.
- Put the goal sheet somewhere where you will see it at least 10 times a day.
- Carry a copy with you; put it on your bedroom door; stick it on your mirror or the refrigerator door.

These simple actions will encourage you to think about your goal, think positively about it, visualize it and speed up the process of getting results. That's what Canadian-born Jim Carrey did – years before he became well known as an actor.

Next Steps

The next section of this book deals with the mental techniques and habits that you need to develop to start yourself on the path to wealth and success as you define it – and keep you on the path, all the way to goal achievement.

Without developing these wealth habits, you could do some amazing planning and still never achieve your potential.

Wealthy people train themselves to "think wealthy". They look for the 'can do', not the 'can't do' in life. They remain open to possibilities and get excited and passionate about the things that interest them.

Luckily, all wealth and success habits can be taught. The first step on the path to wealth is self-knowledge. We have covered this in Part One, which means that you're already on your way.

Now it's time to move on to the next step: Learning to Think Wealthy.

PART TWO:

The Universal Laws

The Universal Laws

15-year-old Carly is back, and here is what she has to say:

Hey everyone! Carly here. Before my Mom and I take you through the Universal Laws, I just wanted to say a couple of things about the work we asked you to do in Part One.

If I hadn't watched my brothers do these exercises with my Mom, I think it might have felt weird or maybe kind of lame to be talking about this kind of stuff with a parent. I mean, nobody talks about how they <u>feel</u> about money – not even with their best friends! And what was even weirder was having my Mom tell me the things she'd thought and felt, too!

So it's because I've been through it myself that I'm pretty sure you spent the last little while thinking 'awright, whatever' and putting down any old thing, just to get the exercise over with. Your mentor might have felt the same way, too. You never know.

What I wanted to say to you now is that you need to go back and look at your answers again. Do it without your mentor if it makes you feel better, just so long as you do it.

Here's why:

Once the strangeness goes away, what it really starts to feel like is that you're part of a team where you get personal coaching every week because you're the *Star Player*. You're practicing to get ready for this big competition, okay? The competition is called Life and the winner gets all this money and control over all the cool things they want to do ... forever!

How you need to look at this book and the exercises in it, is like your regular team practice sessions. In any practice, there are always these warm-up exercises you have to do so your muscles can take the pressure you're about to put on them, right?

Okay, so it's the same thing here: Part One of *the Wealthy Teen* is your warm-up drill. You have to get your brain muscles ready for the daily workout you're going to make it do, to get you rich in every way.

That's all I wanted to say about that. Go back and look at your answers. If you blew it off, take the time to tell the truth. You'll be glad you did. And by the way? Writing it all down really helps. Seriously!

See ya!

Carly's right.

We're moving on to some exciting ideas that have to do with the opportunities that are waiting for you. We know you'll be glad you've taken the time to get yourself in the right frame of mind.

Here we go...

The Universal Law of Attraction

The Universal Law of Attraction states that we attract to us whatever we focus our thoughts, feelings, energy and attention on.

If we are constantly talking trash (negative thoughts) and complaining (negative feelings), negative people and things will be what we attract. That type of negative person comes around and always finds a way to give us plenty to complain about. That's the Law of Attraction: You focused on that kind of people and you got ... them.

Likewise, if we are too lazy to put our minds and bodies to their best use – acting, thinking and feeling positive and optimistic and goal-oriented – we will attract dull, lazy, mediocre people who have even less ambition than we do. We will sit around getting fat and stupid together. That's the Law of Attraction: You focused on that and you got ... that.

On the other hand, if we have a goal that we are excited about – one that we focus our best efforts to reach – opportunities will continue to present themselves that will bring us closer to that goal every day. That's the Law of Attraction, too: You focused on that and you got ... that.

Remember, then. The Law of Attraction doesn't discriminate about good or bad. Whatever you focus on, it brings you *that*.

The best way to prove this to yourself is to set a goal to "say nothing negative to anyone for one whole day". No matter what happens, look for a way to say something positive when.... You missed the bus and that made you late ... You forgot an assignment ... You lost your pocket money because there was a hole in your pocket you kept forgetting to mend ... Some joker tries to get a rise out of you by bullying or insulting you.

No matter what upset you, instead of complaining about your bad luck and reliving the negativity of the moment all day, think to yourself, "I will say nothing negative to anyone for one whole day, no matter what." Say to others, "This taught me a lesson I'll never forget – it was worth doing for a whole day."

If you manage to get through a whole day without negative talk, try it for a second day. If you succeed, try for one more day. Work on it until you can go a whole week without indulging in those mental 'pity parties' that keep you so focused on the bad stuff you have no time to see the good.

If you can spend a whole week in positive gear, a curious thing will happen: You'll realize that all those negative people you used to spend time with? They are really pretty boring. They never have anything new to say because they're always stuck on something that went wrong yesterday. They're never interested in doing anything fun – they're way too busy looking for ways to pick things apart and ruin a good time for everyone else.

Pretty soon you'll be too busy to hang out with them: You'll be having way too much fun being positive, focused on a really cool goal, or just smiling all the time. And you will attract more ... of that!

The Universal Law of Money

Money is really like people. Consider this: You bad-mouth and complain about a person that you'd really like to date ... or have as your mentor ... or just spend more time with. Is your negativity going to attract to you or chase away this person?

Ah. If it were you, you'd be running in the other direction, right? And so does that person.

Money is the same. Complain about it. It stays away.

But even more than that, the Universal Law of Money states that money only comes to those who recognize its value.

This means that you have to learn to respect money (that is, not complain...).

How do you do that? By being happy that you have some!

You also express respect for money by taking care of it; by thinking before you spend it; by making sure you spend it on things that you really need or want. You also keep it organized in your wallet!

You don't throw it away on things that are not good value. You don't borrow it unless and until you have a plan in place to pay it back as quickly as you can.

Imagine that every dollar you get is like a drop of rain. If it only rains for a few minutes every now and then, it doesn't take long for the drops to disappear and leave the ground dry again. If it rains really hard for a short time, the ground can't soak it up fast enough and the extra just runs away. Before you know it, the ground is dry again.

Now imagine yourself as someone who respects the value of the rain. You get a big container with a secure lid. When it starts to rain, you take the lid off the container, you put it right under the gutter spout, and watch the rainwater gush in. When it stops raining, you put the lid back on the container to keep the water from evaporating. Whenever you want to water your plants or your lawn, you don't have to wait for it to rain. You can go to your container and take out just enough to make everything green again.

You can't control <u>how</u> the rain falls, but you <u>can</u> control what you do with it when it falls. Let it run off in streams or dry up. Capture it, and treat it like the precious commodity that it is.

In the same way, you may not be able to control <u>how</u> your money comes to you, but you <u>can</u> control what you do with it when it comes. Just as you found a container for your rainwater, you can put the money you get into safe places and let it work for you even when you sleep. Then it will be there for you when you need it most.

Learning to respect money means that you give it every opportunity to grow bigger and stronger so that it can work harder for you.

The Pennies from Heaven

> One of our friends is a great "Urban Hiker." She is always out for a walk. And she always comes home with her pocket jingling with coins she's picked up on her walks. When she sees a coin, she is truly, deeply delighted. It is that energy of delight – as positive and joyful as it is – that the Law of Money is attracted to.

Delight is a very different energy from craving. One of the hardest things to learn is how to control those sudden cravings for things that make you want to throw your money away the very first chance you get. But you can do it. All you need is a schedule and a plan.

For instance, let's say you can't resist buying the newest fashion or car magazine every month. You can still have your monthly 'fix' without spending as much: Get a couple of friends to pool money to pay for the magazines, then share them amongst yourselves. After you've done that for a few months, you'll have enough money *saved* so that you and your friends can buy a subscription to the magazine that offers big discounts off the monthly cover price.

Suppose your favorite magazine costs $3.00. Your plan might look like this:

```
Cost of one monthly magazine  = $ 3.00
Cost per person per year       = $36.00


Cost shared between 3 people  = $ 1.00
Cost per person per year       = $12.00
```

Each of you saves $24 in one year.

Now suppose that $3.00 magazine is available at a 3-year subscription discount of 50% [3 x $36 = $108 x 50%], or $54.

```
Cost of a three-year subscription       = $54.00
Cost per person (3 x $18 = $54)  = $18.00
```

But each of you saved $24 that first year. That means you can each pay for your share of the subscription and still have money left over.

See what happens when you put a plan in motion to get money to work for you? In the first year, you saved enough money by sharing with your friends to pay for a three-year subscription! If you took the $3 you normally spent on the magazine every month and put it away in a jar, at the end of that 3-year period you'd have $108 plus the $6 left over from the $24 you had saved in the first year. That's a total of $116 because you managed your money and put it to work for you!

Multiply the opportunities to do this. Look around. Maybe you and a sibling wear the same sizes of clothing. You can share some of them, perhaps. You like music; you can pool with friends on downloads or real CD purchases. Look for savings opportunities.

This is why people say "Money is power and Wealth is energy." And as the savings accumulate, take a moment to feel that delight and joy!

Money is Power

The greatest power money has is <u>not</u> the ability to buy anything you want. This is what we think in the early days of examining our beliefs and habits about money.

Money is the power that comes with the <u>freedom</u> it gives you to make the choices you want, based on the money you have.

Wealth is Energy

To be wealthy you must learn to hold onto your money and spend it wisely. The financially wise say, "It's not so much how much money you make that's important – but how much you keep."

You must be energized with purpose so that you achieve your full potential. Having money that you have kept, so that you can take advantage of a future opportunity is freedom to make choices. Having choices energizes you with unlimited potential.

Challenging Experiences Energize and Empower

The greatest challenge you face when you unlock the energy to achieve your purpose and reach your potential is the change you must make in the way you live your life.

Each journey begins with a single step. Your journey begins when you shift your attitude out of 'idle' and put your mind in forward gear. Just like in a 4-speed vehicle, you start making changes in first gear. You have a success. You shift into 2nd gear. Another success, and you move into 3rd gear and so on. Unless you are willing to change and grow, you will remain exactly where you are, spinning your wheels and wasting your resources.

When you take your future – and this includes your wealth – in your hands, you are telling the universe, "I am ready to trust myself and my ability to take care of my funds".

This stretching – overcoming your fear to achieve something that will help make you financially free – is what power is all about.

Money Comes When You Call

Nature has a way of maintaining a universal balance in all things. Most of us cannot see this cause/effect relationship because we're standing too close. But let's look at something you <u>have</u> seen before.

Think of a dollar amount that you typically need to get through a given month. The parent reading this thinks of the total of all monthly bills and expenses. The teen thinks perhaps of gas for their car (or for using dad's car), snack money, cash for an item of clothing.

Now remember how often has that *exact amount* found its way to you just in time. That's right! Money often appears when we need it, in the exact amount that we have in mind. And we never question it. We are so busy dealing with the next disaster, that we never see the pattern or the balance that is maintained. We never put it together that, having asked the universe to send $X, $X is exactly the amount we receive so that we are able to stay in our familiar comfort zone.

There is nothing wrong with being comfortable, if being comfortable is all you want to be. But it isn't likely that you will ever get wealthy while being "comfortable" with exactly what you have now. You will be too comfortable to welcome the idea of working to enable change and growth.

Good versus Not Good

In many ways we have been brainwashed to believe that the power and energy inherent in wealth are unworthy goals to reach for. Our society places such great importance on being comfortable that it is considered rude to say you want to have the power to enable change and growth. Some people believe having too much money is bad.

Yet how can money be bad? Money is nothing more than a few pieces of paper made with paper and ink, nothing more than a few coins made with metals of some value. Money is a means to an end, a tool for exchange. We trade our time and our talent for money to pay the bills and enhance the quality of material life. Our surplus money feeds the poor and helps charities make a meaningful difference to millions.

In spite of this, people insist that a life spent in pursuit of money is bad; that our time and energy are better spent in being kind. They tell us that it is love that makes the world go round, not the money that loving people can use for a greater good.

The fact is that money by itself is neither good nor bad. It is of value to the person who understands its uses and puts it to work. Used wisely, it can afford you a membership to the gym, the chance to help someone in need, the joy of eating a good meal, the humility of giving to charity, and the pleasure of the world we live in. It can provide opportunities to enrich our lives and those of our children.

Because we listen to the people who tell us money is bad, we fear the consequences of having more than 'enough'. Imagine what might happen if we got over our fear of asking for more than 'enough'; of dreaming big!

What do you suppose might happen if we stopped praying our limiting prayers: "I just need $X thousand to pay my bills!"

What do you think the outcome might be if we said something like, "Help me double my income this year so that money problems are a thing of the past and I can do all the things I need to do – including donating to the charity I have always wanted to help."

What happens is that money begins to flow, as long as you take action.

After we make a conscious decision to accept the responsibility of having it enter our lives, and make a plan, money flows in a constant stream, filling our lives with abundance. Unlike the people who win the lottery and promptly spend every dime, we have to be prepared to set goals and do the work to make sure that the changes happen on our terms.

There are two things we must do to invite the power of money and the energy of wealth into our lives:

1. First, ask for money, and take appropriate action
2. Then get prepared to do what it takes to use it wisely.

The Universal Law of Abundance

The Law of Abundance states that there is always enough. Enough of anything and everything we need. Always.

Scarcity versus Abundance

No matter where we look, the business of living is all around us. In any trade, whether it is that of a plumber, a painter, a lawyer, a bricklayer, a designer, there is work to be done. And for the good worker, there is so much work that's it's difficult to do it all.

How many houses are sold in one day? How many gallons of fuel consumed, how many loaves of bread baked, how many shares traded, how many clothes bought, hairstyles created?

In spite of the clear proof of abundance, our culture teaches us to focus on scarcity. We are encouraged to see the glass half-empty rather than half-full. We are trained to believe that happiness can only be realized when our cravings are satisfied: when our need to consume the greatest quantity rather than the finest quality is met.

How many times in a day do people bemoan the lack of material objects in their lives? How many people truly believe that their happiness is a function of buying, getting, having that vacation, that TV, that car, that coat, those shoes? How many times have we not bought a food or clothing item because we've judged it "beyond our means" and tell our family "we can't afford it"?

Have we ever taken the time to list all the things we <u>do</u> have? When you consider the alternative, the fact that we are alive – that we can think and feel and have freedom of choice – is the greatest "have" of all. After that, everything else is a bonus.

Measuring Abundance

Can we count the raindrops when it rains? Can we grab onto those drops with our hands? The answer is no. But if we hold our hands palm up to the rain, those raindrops will fill our hands to overflowing.

In the same way, the Universe is filled with abundance. No matter what our field of work might be, or what we want to do with our lives, the ability to do it well and reap the rewards exists. All we have to do is reach out and take hold of the opportunities that life provides. Our responsibility is to commit to a plan of action and follow it.

Imagine a life of abundance working in the field of your choice.

- What do you need to DO to achieve the success you desire?
- Where do you want to BE six months or a year from now?
- How do you PLAN to get there?

Think about the baby steps you can take. Can you research your idea? Can you talk to people about it? If you see this as the work that will provide the life you are seeking, you will make the time to chart a course. Take time, analyze your opportunities and then act on them. Do something every day to bring you closer to your goals. Success can be yours if you are willing to work for it.

Remember that there is no such thing as an 'overnight' success.

- Warren Buffett became extremely wealthy. But over 20 and 30 years of patient investing!
- Adele became very popular as a singer. But she worked for it all the years of her teens in music classes and voice and composition training!

Give and Receive

The Universal Law of Abundance works when we recognize the responsibility each of us shares and the rewards that come from putting our money to work. We must place a proper value on the contribution that we make to society.

People who are taught that it is better to give than to receive, often think that reaching for a personal goal is a selfish thing and therefore wrong. What they fail to do is consider the balance inherent in the give-and-take equation. When we take something, we give as well.

Consider a $10 bill given as a gift. The person who receives the gift exchanges the money for food. The grocer takes the ten dollars, gives half of it to charity and spends the rest. The people who receive the money – whether as charity or in exchange for a service or the sale of goods – go on to spend it and give it in turn. As long as the bill is in circulation, it will keep on bringing value to those who take it and pass it along.

The original value of that $10 bill multiplies with every exchange. If that single $10 bill has so much power over the lives of so many, think of the Potential value $100 would create in the marketplace. What of the potential value $1,000, $10,000 or $100,000 represents?

The Abundance Model at Work

In order to recognize the thinking habits we unconsciously apply, we need to look outside our own lives and examine the actions of a stranger.

Example:

Meet Sheena: Sheena is a singer who is good at her work. When Sheena applied the 'scarcity' model in managing her career ...

> *"I need one more booking this month to survive. Just one! I am going for an audition and I have to get it. If I don't, I've had it"...*

... she found enough work to get by and nothing more.

One day, Sheena heard about the 'abundance' model and decided to give it a try. The first thing she did was write down a belief statement about her talent and her place in an abundant world. The statement looked like this:

> *"Everyone loves to listen to my beautiful songs. There is work for the taking; all I have to do is decide to tap into the market. There are many ways of doing what I love and earning good money. When I go for this audition, it isn't a life or death situation because if I don't get this job, I will get the next one."*

As long as she wanted to work as a singer and sing her heart out, guess how many jobs she got? Sheena got each and every one that she tried for. Her success rate was an incredible 100%!

How Did This Happen? Why Did It Work?

When Sheena approached her work from an abundance perspective, the universe bent over backwards to fill her demand. She did her best work when she was able to remain relaxed about the outcome. There was a calm serenity that emanated from her and reached out to embrace her audience. They could sense that she was stress-free and doing something because she wanted to, not because it represented a dollar value in her head.

Because her energy was positive, people were drawn to her. Sheena got all the work she wanted and ended up creating a successful album, making her music available to an even larger audience. She worked hard to reach her goal, knowing that you have to make the contacts to get the work. She chose to believe in herself and act accordingly, knowing that anything less is standing in the way of success.

As mentors, we need to learn the abundance model and share this belief with our teens. Teens need to share this model – this belief in abundance – with their peers. We need to respect the Universal Law of Abundance and learn to ask for the things we need, then follow up with enthusiastic and passionate action!

The Universal Law of Passion

Ever heard of people wanting to "do the work they love", but hesitating because they might not earn enough doing it? Sure, you have. We even spoke about this earlier when we discussed potential and what you love to do.

The Universal Law of Passion states that the quality of your passion is reflected in the quality of the work that you do. And passion is linked to abundance. Passion is linked to doing something *well*.

Though passion manifests itself in different ways, when passion is real it shines from a person's eyes, investing energy in everything they do. When you feel passionate about something, it is reflected in the quality of the work that you do and the energy you bring to it.

You can pretend to be passionate about something. Other people can pretend to believe in your passion. But the Universe knows the truth, just as you do. Even those around you know when something is not quite as it should be.

The Universe provides us with a never-ending abundance of opportunity. For every person who dislikes a job, there is someone out there that would love to do it! There are passionate high-rise window washers, big-city dog walkers, cleaners, quilt-makers and landscapers... And that is only people's professions. When you add their hobbies to the list, well! People are passionate about their hobbies, too, aren't they?

All of them have an opportunity to do well because society needs all kinds of people to do all types of jobs...and have all kinds of hobbies.

Each of us has a role to play in making the world a better place. When we give a part of ourselves to the world, unafraid, we stretch to our full potential. Passion is an integral part of success. It is what takes us to the top. Unless we are passionate in doing the things we believe in, wealth will not follow. When we are? Abundance comes to us like metal to a magnet!

Passion versus Fear

Passion can be very frightening to those who have lived their lives by the scarcity model. Fear produces anger, as can be seen in this response from a parent who cannot cope with his teen's passion:

> *"You want to be a stained glass artist? Are you nuts? That's not a real job! What kind of a future will you have? How will you feed your family? Who will carry on our family business? Your marks are good enough to get an MBA. Why would you throw a good career away?"*

You can substitute any number of 'unorthodox' creative pursuits for the 'stained glass' in this example. The point is that a parent who lives by the *scarcity model* is too afraid to see any practical future for a son who is determined to follow his passion instead of the path his father chose. Instead of opportunity, the father sees failure; instead of encouraging his son to find a practical way to follow his dream, he digs in his heels to defend the choices he made when he was young. He tries to burden his son with guilt and responsibility instead of helping him balance both sides of his life.

There are a number of ways this scenario can play out:

- If the son is *somewhat* passionate about stained glass, he might do the MBA and be happy enough with it as a part-time hobby.
- If he is *truly* passionate, he will either bend to his father's will and be miserable until he goes back to his first love, or
- If he is strong enough and has confidence in himself, he might ignore his father's advice and go for a career in stained glass, or
- The teen may complete the MBA and work part-time at stained glass until he is ready to decide on his career.

To the ordinary eye, a stained glass business doesn't look really promising. It will be hard work until the young man learns the skill and establishes a name.

Let's look at the example from each of our two models. The Scarcity model might sound something like this:

> *"He'll be lucky to sell enough to make ends meet."*

The Abundance model might sound like this:

> *"He'll be accomplished in his field. He may invent a new method or a new glaze and become a 'hot' artist. He might make one-of-a-kind pieces, pack them beautifully and start exporting them to countries where no stained glass is available (hiring the workers he needs). He might specialize in recreating old stained glass that may be damaged, destroyed or lost."*

When passion is married to action and perseverance, the result is a feeling of joy in your creative endeavors and satisfaction in a job well done. You don't have to be an artist to be a success. As long as you are passionate about the work you do and willing to take ownership of all that it demands, success can be yours!

What are you passionate about? Make a list here:

1. --
   ----
2. --
   ----
3. --
   ----
4. --
   ----
5. --

Discuss what you have been and currently are passionate about. Record your main points here.

The Universal Law of Luck

The Universal Law of Luck states that good fortune comes to those who work at it.

Let's analyze luck first. What is it exactly? The dictionary describes luck as *'the events or circumstances that operate for or against an individual'.*

In other words, luck is more than winning at cards or betting on the right horse or winning the lottery. While those are examples of good fortune, they are based on random chance rather than determined action. How many fortunes do you think were built on random chance or luck such as that? I don't know anyone who built a fortune by winning a lottery. Nor do I know anyone who knows anyone who has done it. In fact, statistics indicate that the money received as lottery winnings disappeared over a period of time.

Our culture considers luck to be something that happens to certain people. The fact is, people aren't born lucky. A little investigation will show that "lucky" folks took some sort of initiative and that their actions inspired their luck. In other words, they made it happen!

Time and time again, stories abound of people who have taken control of their destinies with a firm hand and gone where they wanted to go. Yes! They were lucky. They were also hard working and willing to do something to get the ball rolling.

Example:

> Kevin's story shows how luck can be driven by determined action. Using part of his savings, Kevin bought some land on the outskirts of the town where he lived. He paid about $50,000 for it and made the mortgage payments over a period of five years. A few years later, he sold the land to a developer for $500,000.

Was Kevin lucky? In a way, yes. Nevertheless, don't you think he *made* his own luck by deciding to buy land in an area that gained in value over time?

If he hadn't thought of it or been open to it, he would never have bought the land. If he hadn't researched the possibilities, he wouldn't have known which piece of land to buy. If he hadn't bought it, he couldn't have sold it.

In other words, if he had thought of it, planned it and researched it but never acted on it, he would never have been lucky. It was the combination of all these factors PLUS his determined action that created his "luck".

We have all heard the success stories of the overnight millionaires selling stocks online. We might consider this to be random chance or luck if we did not know how much work these individuals contributed to make it happen: all the research they had to do before they bought the stock;

the hours they spent, monitoring the progress of those stocks to determine the right time to sell; the courses they may have taken related to buying and selling stocks online.

How can you help your teens become lucky ... or make more of their own luck?

- Recognize their passions and abilities.
- Encourage their interests.
- Get involved and support them with teachers, coaches or classes.
- Give insight on what you know about their passion.
- Set them up to speak with someone to further their knowledge.
- Recognize things that they do well and enjoy doing.

By nurturing their talents and encouraging them, you will help them gain the confidence and ability to succeed in any avenue of life. By inviting them to share their dreams, you will excite their passion and inspire their action.

Speak to your teens and ask them what they feel their talents are. Ask them what they would like to be doing and where they would like to be in 1 year ... or in 10 years. Plan ten mutual goals to accomplish in the next five years as a means to familiarize them with the process of setting goals and planning ahead. Be sure the ten goals you set out are fun and make a sincere commitment to achieve them.

The Universal Law of Persistence

The Universal Law of Persistence states that to be successful and wealthy, you need the will to carry on carrying on! This means dealing with negativity from other people, staying passionate about your dream and remaining focused on the end goal. You are the one who keeps yourself going, moving toward that goal.

Look at anyone who has achieved success. They never let up. They were *relentless* in their pursuit of contacts, education and new skills – anything that could help them move forward.

When one door closes, another one is already open

Life can be viewed like a magnificent mansion that contains many hallways and corridors. If you are trying to reach a special room, you have many different routes you can take. For every door that closes, another one opens. While the routes may be different, they all reach the same destination. Preparing for setbacks and maintaining goals in the face of adversity is a primary life skill that we – as responsible adults – should practice ourselves and teach our children.

Remind yourself of your ultimate goals: Be relentless in your pursuit of them each and every day.

The important thing to remember is that adversity is not always a force working on us from the outside. More often than not, it is our own fears – including our uncertainties about money and wealth – that stand in the way of our success. Sit down with your teen and discuss what makes each of you nervous about money and wealth. Think about the goals you may have formed earlier in your life and try to identify the things that may have hindered you from reaching your goal. Write them down. Ask your teens how they would deal with any problems, concerns or fears they can think of right now.

Past Goals for Mentors

1. --
   ----
2. --
   ----
3. --
   ----
4. --
   ----
5. --

Why didn't you achieve these goals? What stopped you or got in the way? What were the circumstances, your own thoughts or ideas that put limitations on you? Write down as much detail as possible.

Mentors, write down in detail why you didn't achieve your goals...

Goal 1: Why I didn't achieve it

Goal 2: Why I didn't make it

Goal 3: What stopped me

Goal 4: What hindered me

Goal 5: What I let get in the way

Now teens, it's your turn:

<u>Past Goals I didn't achieve</u>

1. ---
----
2. ---
----
3. ---
----
4. ---
----
5. ---

Why didn't you achieve these goals? What stopped you or got in the way? What were the circumstances, your own thoughts or ideas that put limitations on you? Write down as much detail as possible.

Teens:

Goal 1: Why didn't I achieve it

Goal 2: What stopped me

Goal 3: Could I have done something to achieve it

Goal 4: Was I committed enough

Goal 5: Was it circumstances

By doing this, you are learning that when problems arrive there are always solutions. At the same time, it is also important to recognize when a plan is flawed and how to cut your losses.

By going through these exercises together, you will help each other learn.

For your teen, it is especially important to know how to deal with adversity *without* your guidance. This is a skill they will need to learn under your care so that they can make it later on their own. Teach them to get excited about new and different ways to resolve problems. Help them enhance their ability to approach problems in new and different ways. Encourage them to think 'outside the box' – in other words, in non-traditional patterns – to solve problems. Give them the tools that promote versatility, build confidence and ease the frustration in high stress situations.

Teach your teens to expect adversity. As I taught my kids with board games when they were little: Sometimes you lose and sometimes you win, but both times? You got to play! You had a chance!

Teach them that problems arrive and bring friends with them, especially when you least expect them. When problems show up, your teens will need to be able to rise to the challenge. With one problem successfully resolved, levels of expectation and confidence rise and when the next problem shows up, it won't cause as much stress as the first. This mental toughness is indispensable if you and your teen want to reach full ⓔ Potential!

To be able to follow the Universal Law of Persistence and maintain your goal no matter what, it helps to know about the two schools of thought that accompany it:

Example:

Whatever happens, happens for the best.

The Universe has a larger plan for us than we can see. If things aren't happening the way we think they should at this moment, it is because something better is waiting in the wings.

Charmaine had always had her heart set on having a magazine for children written by children. She did the research, gathered the facts and found the investment money. Just when it seemed that her dream would come true, the investor pulled the plug and Charmaine was left with nothing. Before she could refinance, a leading newspaper launched a magazine based on the same concept.

She did her best to comfort herself with the Abundance Theory, telling herself that whatever happened was for the best. Believing that the world was filled with opportunities, she felt certain that something better was sure to head her way. She did not give up her dream.

Six months later, Charmaine set up her own publishing company. The research she had done to launch the children's magazine gave her the tools she needed to establish the new business. The mistakes she had made in her first venture taught her valuable lessons that put her on solid ground for her second. The crushing disappointment she had experienced made her realize the need for a healthy perspective and taught her to respect herself as an individual with a life beyond the business. Looking back over the events of the previous year,

Charmaine had this to say:

"Obstacles are everywhere, but so are opportunities! Even in the midst of my disappointment, I knew that something better was sure to come along. When my magazine idea went down the drain, I looked for another."

Nothing that you ever do is wasted.

Charmaine's hard work came in handy in a different way than she first envisioned. The same is true for you: knowledge is always there in the back of your mind, waiting for an opportunity to help you down the road. What you do today always leads to something new tomorrow. Be patient, be positive and be persistent. Focus relentlessly on your goals!

Most of us know someone who lost a job and used that life-changing event as an opportunity to start something they had always wanted to do. By bringing their experiences and skills to bear, they forged ahead and helped themselves to the abundance that is freely available in the world ... if one only knows where to look.

The Universal Law of Giving Back

The Universal Law of Giving Back states that whatever you give will return to you 10-fold.

There is no doubt that it is a privilege to be alive in this place in time. Those of us who live in North America are so much wealthier than 90% of the population living on the planet that we have a moral obligation to give both time and money to those less fortunate. We have a moral obligation not to moan and groan about "how little" we have.

The reason you give back is to maintain the give-and-take balance in the Universe. Because your gift returns to you 10-fold, the principle of **tithing** is to give 10% of your net worth away. The choice is yours to make when it comes to the beneficiary of your gift.

Carly, Matt, Dru and I like to support those who inspire us to become better people. We sit down as a family and discuss the ways we plan to give each year. Sometimes we support a person who works at our church; other times we pick people we admire in the community who do great things. You can also give to a charity organization. For many people the amount they give to charity is over and above the amount they tithe.

You may wonder: "*What if I can't give 10% right now?*" My answer to that is to give what you can and make a commitment to work your way up to 10% or more.

There is an old saying:

Every time someone helps you unexpectedly, it is a good deed you have done that has come back to you.

The idea of giving and helping is based on the belief that life is circular; that what goes around comes back. Based on that theory alone, if each of us were to help one person, there would be no needy people left in this world.

Meaningful giving also completes us as human beings. We may think it makes no difference if we give, but it does: The difference is in you. Every effort you make for others makes you feel blessed. Think of all the research made possible by donations, all the clothes provided to the needy, all the food banks and the charities that are improving the quality of peoples' lives thanks to your generosity. If you can't spare cash, give time. See the difference in you.

Remember that every little drop counts. If there were no little drops, there would be no big ocean!

Applying the Universal Laws

When you apply the principles of these Universal Laws, you begin to think in an entirely new way. As you think differently, your attitudes and actions change. In a very short time, you adopt the beliefs and develop the behaviors that invite wealth and abundance into your life.

Taken together, this new set of skills will change you. You will no longer be content with an 'okay', 'middling', 'comfortable' existence. You will be excited by the challenge that growth and change bring to your life. As you learn to apply these new skills, you will achieve a life free of debt and worry and set your teens on the path to wealth and prosperity as well.

These 'abundant' attitudes and beliefs, combined with the money managing techniques that are laid out in Part III, provide the blueprint for your financial future.

Go back to Part One and see what you have written down.

- Has your thinking changed since then?
- What does the new 'You' want now?
- Are you still content with crumbs instead of a big, gooey slice?
- What about the whole cake?

The Universal Life Lessons

1. The Glass Half Full

Wealthy people believe in abundance. They believe that life, money and success is theirs for the taking. They know they have to reach out and grasp it. They play the Life game to win. They focus on the glass half full and on the rain overflowing the palm of their hands. They hold their hands out to fate and fate fills it.

Example:

> At the age of twenty-five, a young woman living in London, England was faced with the tragic death of her mother after she had lost her battle with a debilitating disease. Her life in turmoil, the young woman took a succession of modest paying jobs, dreaming all the while of a life in which power came to you for the asking and enabled you to live a fantastic existence. She married and divorced a young man while she was living in a foreign country. She returned home with an infant daughter. She was unable to support herself and went on public assistance. While her daughter took her afternoon naps, the young woman began to write, infusing her dreams of power, fantastic adventure and unlimited freedom into her words.

Four years later, the young woman published her first novel and the world was introduced to a very, very famous Wizard for the first time.

Twenty years later? She is happily remarried; she is a billionaire and philanthropist ... and is still writing novels.

What about you?

Do you focus on the things you don't have and how you might never have them? If that is what you do and that is what you are teaching your teens, you are creating a legacy of scarcity for you and for them.

To achieve abundance, you have to believe it can happen before the opportunities will present themselves to you.

Author J.K. Rowling is the young woman in our story. Her series of books about the young Wizard Harry Potter has enchanted the world.
As she sat writing every day, she focused on success. *Relentlessly.* Because she knew she had a great story. But what is more, she <u>knew</u> she was a *great story-teller!* She had faith that everything was going to work out for her. She saw a better life than the one she was living as she wrote.

2. Rags to Riches

Every action in the Universe has an equal and opposite reaction. Wealthy people take action and make life work for them.

Example:

> A young boy traveled to India from his home in Nepal. He was from a poor family, had hardly any education and lived in the house of an advertising executive. To pay for his room and board, he got up at 5 a.m. to do chores before going to work as a clerk in the executive's advertising office. Every night he did more chores for the family before going to bed at 11 p.m.
>
> In spite of the long hours he worked, he still managed to study and complete high school. English was his second language and he knew that in order to succeed he would have to improve. He began to practice and with the help of some willing friends and people around the office, he was completely fluent in just one year.
>
> At the same time, he made it a point to learn as much as he could at the office, turning down no job he was asked to do. His consistent efforts were rewarded with more and more responsible jobs as he proved

his worth. In time, he became Vice President of one of the largest advertising firms in the world.

If he had never taken those first steps to educate himself and change his life, he would still be a lowly, impoverished clerk fetching coffee, making photocopies and doing deliveries. If he had said to himself, "*What chance can there be for someone like me?*" he would never have seen the opportunities that were waiting for him. However, he didn't let the hardships he faced stop him from achieving his goal. He reacted to his circumstances by focusing on what he could do to change them. He learned that by making incredible efforts to succeed, the Universe would reward him with incredible success.

What type of person are you? Do you find it difficult to adapt to new situations or do you see a detour for every roadblock? Work with your teen to list five examples when each of you reacted well and badly to changing situations. Discuss them with your teen.

Mentor: Five times I reacted well to a situation...

Situation 1:---

My Reaction: --

Why it was a good reaction: ------------------------------------
----

Situation 2:---

My Reaction: --

Why it was a good reaction: ------------------------------------
----

Situation 3: ---

My Reaction: ---

Why it was a good reaction: --

Situation 4: ---

My Reaction: ---

Why it was a good reaction: --

Situation 5: ---

My Reaction: --

Why it was a good reaction: ---------------------------------------
----

Mentor: Five times I reacted badly to a situation...

Situation 1:--

My Reaction: --

Why it was a bad reaction: --

Situation 2:--

My Reaction: --

Why it was a bad reaction: --

Situation 3:--

How I reacted: --

Why it was a bad reaction: ----------------------------------
----

Situation 4:--

How I reacted: --

Why it was a bad reaction: ----------------------------------
----

Situation 5:--

How I reacted: ---

Why it was a bad reaction: -------------------------------------
----

Now analyze them and look for things you did well, or could have done better. Write your summary here.

Teen: Five times I reacted well to a situation...

Situation 1:---

My Reaction: ---

Why it was a good reaction: ---------------------------------------
----

Situation 2:---

How I reacted: ---

Why it was a good reaction: ---------------------------------------
----

Situation 3:--

How I reacted: --

Why it was a good reaction: ------------------------------

Situation 4:--

How I reacted: --

Why it was a good reaction: ------------------------------

Situation 5:--

My Reaction: --

Why it was a good reaction: -----------------------------------
----

Teen: Five times I reacted badly to a situation...

Situation 1:--

My Reaction: --

Why it was a bad reaction: --

Situation 2:--

How I reacted: --

Why it was a bad reaction: --

Situation 3:---

How I reacted: ---

Why it was a bad reaction: ---------------------------------

Situation 4:---

How I reacted: ---

Why it was a bad reaction: ---------------------------------


```
Situation 5: -----------------------------------------------
-------------------------------------------------------------
-------------------------------------------------------------
How I reacted: ----------------------------------------------
-------------------------------------------------------------
-------------------------------------------------------------
-------------------------------------------------------------
-------------------------------------------------------------
Why it was a bad reaction: ----------------------------------
-------------------------------------------------------------
-------------------------------------------------------------
-------------------------------------------------------------
```

As a teen and as a mentor, how well do you react to change?

Change is a part of life. It happens every day. Anyone who cannot adjust and adapt to changing situations cannot reach their full ⓔ Potential. For example, even as an individual you change as grow older. Growth is a natural part of change. For a person to be successful, he or she must have a positive attitude about change.

To help you see how you cope with change, write down any
<u>Five Specific Situations</u> that have required you to change:

<u>Five specific situations</u> that have required you to change:

1..

2..

3..

4..

5..

Do you see a pattern in how you dealt with change in those
examples? Give an example of how do you *prefer to* deal
with change. What is your first reaction? Is it solution-
oriented? Do you automatically resist having to change?

_____

_____

_____

_____

_____

_____

3. Short Term Pain versus Long Term Gain

Wealthy people not only believe in their Potential for wealth, they are committed to creating wealth.

They don't expect things to fall into their lap; they work hard at making things happen. They understand that it takes hard work and commitment to achieve the goals they have set; that it takes time, patience and sacrifice.

There may be times when you have to spend weekends, holidays and evenings to reach your goal. You need to be prepared to do what may not always be fun or easy to get there. You need to think in terms of 'short-term pain for long-term gain.'

Example:

A young girl enjoys working with beads. As her skill grows and her ideas mature, she begins making necklaces and other jewelry. Her parents support her sense of entrepreneurship by encouraging her to create different designs. They discuss various ways her hobby might produce an income and offer to advance her the supplies she needs. To help her understand fiscal responsibility, they show her how to set up a plan to repay the money they loaned her to buy supplies.

The girl loves working with beads and even though she misses out on the occasional outing with her friends, she is excited by the goal she has set for herself and is willing to make the sacrifice. She wants to sell her necklaces and puts some money towards a website where she can market her work to the world.

To achieve lasting success and happiness, you must choose something you enjoy doing. Without passion, you may find yourself less motivated to get where you want to go. Teaching our teens that in order to be truly happy you must love your work can be easy to overlook. Spend time discussing things that make them happy. By focusing attention on what makes them happy, you may find creative new ways to help them achieve their financial goals while having fun.

By encouraging passion and an entrepreneurial spirit, we can help our children adopt a positive attitude that will carry them into their adult lives. Encouraging them to develop an entrepreneurial spirit can be as simple as a setting up a roadside lemonade stand or working together fixing cars and selling them. Recognize your teens' strong points and help develop them.

Mountains and Molehills

People who are in financial distress can easily consider themselves to be living in the shadow of a mountain of debt. It takes an attitude of abundance to realize that their current situation is nothing more than a temporary setback: a molehill they can eventually overcome.

Until they adopt the attitude of abundance, they will remain stuck where they are: believing that being 'wealthy' is something you are 'born' with. It won't do any good to tell them that the number of self-made millionaires is growing every day. They will remain convinced that wealth is a matter of destiny: that if it's in your destiny to be wealthy, you will be.

People are created to succeed but nothing is served on a silver platter. The Universe has a worm for every bird, but it doesn't just throw it in the nest! You have to go out and find your worms. You have to be prepared to go out and get what you want! This is how you create your own luck.

Are you willing to do what it takes to create wealth for yourself and your family? You won't get there until you take the first step and commit you heart, your skill and expertise to being wealthy. The longest journey begins with a single step. The best book you ever read began with one word. One step, one word... and a commitment to finish what you start.

4. Opportunities and Obstacles

One of the differences between wealthy people and those who struggle lies in the way they view the road ahead.

Example:

Two little girls set up a lemonade stand at the end of their driveway. After a while, their big brother notices that no one is stopping or even slowing down. He takes a walk to see where everyone is going and comes back with the news that a big sale is being held on the lawn at the church around the corner.

While the youngest starts to cry, the oldest girl thinks for a moment and then goes and speaks to her mother. In a few minutes, she returns with her brother's wagon. She helps her sister climb inside, loading lemonade supplies and chairs around her. She asks her brother to pull the wagon to the new location. He laughs and tells her she's wasting her time and the youngest girl cries even harder. The older girl pulls the wagon to the church by herself and the two girls set up shop.

Within an hour, they've sold all their lemonade and the Minister's wife has offered them each a big piece of pie.

While others see insurmountable obstacles, people with an attitude of abundance see hurdles they have to jump over to move on. When wealthy people are given an opportunity, the first thing they do is create a plan to make it work for them.

Which category would you rather be in?

We are influenced by our peers. Their negative attitudes can cause us to doubt ourselves. Why are they negative? The main reason is because they have a hard time accepting change. When they hear about the challenge you are facing, they know you will change. They may want you to succeed, but won't want your relationship to suffer. They will do what they can to prevent that from happening, even if it means ruining your dreams. Be sure you take their criticism as constructive. Don't let them tell you that it cannot be done.

Be a friend who has a supportive, positive, glass-half-full attitude. Support your friends and they'll support you back – positively.

Ask everyone in your family to get involved in your goal. Ask them to help you by reading this book and supporting your efforts. Create a real team spirit to set the stage for long-term success. Do this and everybody wins in the end.

5. The Forest Hidden in the Trees

People can be so busy searching outside themselves for answers that they fail to see the opportunities that exist right in front of them.

Example:

Terry has been teaching English as a private tutor, taking two students at a time and receiving $X per session in return. She loves her work, but the money she makes doesn't pay her bills. So Terry looks for a better way to market her skills.

After doing some research, Terry discovers that she has the qualifications to work at an ESL school, where English is taught as a second language. She now teaches 20 people in a class and has 3 classes a day. She spends no time advertising for students and doesn't have to worry when one of them cancels a class. She also gets a very good bonus and benefits package through the school.

But she didn't stop there!

Everyone tells Terry that she has a special gift when it comes to teaching. Terry decides to create a home study course that will allow students to practice her techniques at home. She records this course on a CD and sells it through the school. Sales are so good that Terry sets up a website and creates a number of different home study courses that she sells online. Before long, her online CD sales revenues are so high that she is able to quit her job at the ESL school. She advertises workshops and seminars on her website and commands very high fees, which people gladly pay.

To be successful, you have to find a way to deliver value to as many people as possible. If you and your teen think small, then small is what is in the future. To achieve success, you must dream big.

What's in a swim? Age is no criteria of success!

Two sixteen year-olds passed their swimming exams and spent the summer teaching others how to swim.

One took a job as a lifeguard at the local community center while the other gave classes in her backyard pool.

Both girls worked hard, but one earned minimum wage at the center, while the other made $15,000 from her backyard!

---

6. The Fish and the Hen

The Fish lays a thousand eggs and never says a word,
The Hen lays one and cackles to the world!

Moral of the story: Advertising pays.

Wealthy people know the value of self-promotion and feel no shyness in promoting themselves or the products and services they offer.

Contrast that with people who like to hold their cards close to their chest. Wealthy people will talk over their plans with everyone they meet. They find it an effective way of networking with like-minded people. It also gives them a chance to practice their selling skills.

Wealthy people can take one good idea and make it work for them while their opposites will have a thousand ideas and no results! No wonder wealthy people are so inspiring and so enthusiastic: When they do something, they commit to it 100%.

Wealthy people apply the same philosophy to their business. They tell anyone and everyone who will listen about what they are doing, why they are doing it and how much fun they are having. Notice that money doesn't come into the picture. Money is a by-product of the immense value they deliver to the masses using their products. Meanwhile, connections are formed, circles completed and growth spurts recorded in their businesses.

If you never tell anyone what you are doing and secrets are your stock in trade, unless you are inventing something new or are a private investigator, not many clients are going to come running to you... for the simple reason that they don't know you exist! Think of all the marketing that happens on-line: Instagram, YouTube, Facebook and Blog sites are only a few examples.

7. Misery Loves Company

People who resent the wealthy wonder how they got 'stinking rich' in the first place. They wait for money to come to them without effort and as a result will always be poor.

Wealthy people admire and appreciate other wealthy and powerful people and seek to learn from them. They behave as though they are already wealthy and actually become wealthy as a result. They are constantly learning and feeling proud, knowing each day is a learning process.

There was a man who was an importer of crabs. Every day he received two crates of crabs from a particular fisherman. The first crate marked P always came open and had exactly 250 crabs. The second crate marked W always came closed and also contained exactly 250 crabs.

Puzzled, the importer asked the fisherman why one crate was covered while the other wasn't. The fisherman replied that the open crate marked P was full of 'poor' crabs while the covered one marked W contained 'wealthy' crabs.

"I don't understand," said the importer. The next day the fisherman sent both crates uncovered. The one marked P had all 250 crabs but the one marked W was empty.

"What happened?" asked the importer. The fisherman replied that the wealthy crabs all admired each other and helped each other to escape. But the poor crabs hated the idea that one of them might do better than the rest. Every time an enterprising crab would try to scuttle to freedom, the others would yank him down and say, *"Just where do you think you are going?"*

Just like the wealthy crabs, if you admire and reach out to wealth, you will feel empowered. If you surround yourself with negative people, chances are you will remain negative yourself. To be wealthy, you have to feel wealthy and change your mode of thinking.

Reach out to successful people you admire. Send them a letter, email or call them to let them know you admire them and tell them why you think they are doing a good job. Send out positive energy and it will come back to you in many different ways. Send out negative energy you will be burdened with negative results.

The Wealthy Duck Theory

If you act like the wealthy, live amongst the wealthy, behave like the wealthy you are much more likely to become wealthy. If it quacks like a duck, walks like a duck, looks like a duck, it's probably a duck!

Misery loves company! What better fun could there be than to have everyone gather around and complain, acting out the role of victim and blaming fate, circumstances and other people for things that did not work out. These negative, unsuccessful people with the Poor crab mentality will never be wealthy. As soon as one decides to break the habit and aim for the top, the others will pull him back.

Positive people know that one negative person can ruin a group of successful high achievers who delight in each other's success.

Whether you are a parent, mentor or a teen, to truly change your mindset? Keep a Success Diary! Begin by identifying the negative thoughts you generate and record every single one that crosses your mind. Even if you only said, "I hate this weather" cross it out and think of a positive way to reframe the sentence. For instance, say instead, "This rain is sure going to make my yard green and gorgeous!"

Do this exercise for each negative thought. This will help you realize how easy it is to fall into negative thinking, by showing you how many such thoughts you are actually having each day!

By rooting out all negative thoughts from your life (by being aware of them and consciously reframing them) you give your body and mind the energy to look for ways to find the positive and let yourself shine.

As your mental energy is set free from its prison of pessimism, positive power will flow through you and you will be able to see the future clearly: where you stand, where you want to go from here ... the answers will become clear.

Many wealthy, powerful people have a personal charisma. Their positive energy is the reason for the magnetic hold they have over so many people. Within five days of building a positive energy field through positive thinking, you will see the difference in yourself and in the way you perceive the world. Within five days, you will start to radiate the serenity and personal power enjoyed by successful people the world over.

In Part III, there is a 30-day game plan that will set you on your road to success. Make sure you follow it. Make a copy for each of you and start it together so you can see who changes faster!

8. If at First You Don't Succeed...

Martial artists know this rule: 'Fall once, Get up once. Fall again, Get up again.'

It is the only way to stay in the fight!

Wealthy people focus their thoughts and their actions on finding solutions to problems. When they hit an obstacle, they may briefly fall back but they quickly regroup and find a way around it. They change, adapt, and find a new way to move forward when it is required. They stay in the fight.

Narrow thinkers and pessimists will see an obstacle looming far ahead and start preparing to fail. There will be game plans and endless talks and they will eventually decide that the obstacle is too big to overcome. It never strikes these people to go around or tunnel under their problems. They will simply give up. They walk away from the fight, saying "I lost."

If we succeed in teaching our teenagers nothing else but this, we will have taught them that "Where there is a will, there is always a way".

9. We Are Not Worthy

A little bird jumped out of the nest and fell to the ground on his very first attempt at flight. The mother bird tut-tutted and carried the baby back to the nest, telling the chick that the next time it would surely fly. But the chick was so upset by his failure he convinced himself he was not good enough; that he would never make it out of the nest alive.

People do this all the time: They make one mistake and punish themselves for the rest of their lives. What's more, they do the same for their family and friends, reminding them every chance they get just how imperfect they are.

Successful people don't limit themselves. They know that any failure is simply one small event in life, and can be managed or turned around or learned from. They also know that failure is a function of success; that every skill takes practice – even the art of being a success. If you can be mentally prepared to fail and try again without blaming yourself, you are more than halfway there.

Successful people believe that the world and everything in it was created for them. They believe that they live in this world to contribute and that it is their duty to let their talents shine: To do well, to bring power and prestige to their world, to help others do equally well. Think of all the foundations and charitable organizations that were established by the wealthy to help the poor.

By giving other people the power to judge us and find us unworthy we give them ownership. We allow them to take away our self-respect and pride. We allow them to limit our success.

Write down your answers to the questions that follow and discuss them in detail. Be honest with each other as you share your life experiences. You are looking for personality traits or characteristics, personal beliefs and the way you think.

Mentors

- Do you think you are unworthy of being successful and wealthy?

- Do you feel that you don't deserve the good things in life?

- Do you feel that the world judges you harshly?

- Do you care what the rest of the world thinks about you?

- Do you have a great need for approval?

- Anything else that you want to add.

Teens

- Do you think you are unworthy of doing well and being wealthy?

- Do you feel that you don't deserve the good that comes your way?

- Do you feel that your friends judge you harshly?

- Do you care what the rest of the world thinks about you?

- Do you have a great need for approval?

- Anything else you want to add.

In this next exercise, write down your own Pros and Cons as well as the Pros and Cons to describe each other. (Pros stands for positive character traits, Cons for the qualities you see as less positive.)

Mentor Sheet – Mentors write down your own Pros and Cons

Pros	Cons
1	
2	
3	
4	
5	
6	
7	
8	
9	
10.	

What assumptions can be made? What kind of job would this person suit? (Example: creative or technology; solitary or group; etc.)

Mentor Sheet – Teens write down your mentor's Pros and Cons

Pros   Cons

1
2
3
4
5
6
7
8
9
10.
Assumptions

Next, we come to the Pros and Cons for Teens.

Teens write down your own Pros and Cons

Pros	Cons
1	
2	
3	
4	
5	
6	
7	
8	
9	
10.	

What is the assumption that can be made about this person's personality strengths? What are the strengths and weaknesses? What would this person do best?

Assumptions

Teen Sheet – Mentors write down your teen's Pros and Cons

Pros	Cons
1	
2	
3	
4	
5	
6	
7	
8	
9	
10.	
Assumptions	

This assessment will help you recognize the strengths and weaknesses in your individual characters. As self-awareness blooms and hidden strengths of character are revealed, your perceptions about your inner selves will change.

Help each other by discussing any issues you might have with your feelings of self-worth. Self-knowledge, love and support go a long way to help you achieve high acceptance levels. They are the key to a successful life filled with the pleasures of realizing our dreams.

10. Wages versus Results

If you get a minimum wage job, no matter how hard you work there is a limit to what you can earn. Even if you are paid more per hour than the minimum, you are still limited in an hourly position – you won't earn more per hour than the amount the employer hired you for.

The goal of wealth (or success) is more difficult to attain when limits are imposed on your ability to earn.

For those whose goal is to achieve success in the short term, slaving at a job that makes money for others in exchange for a predetermined wage or salary isn't good enough. The person in search of success is looking for a way to have their money work harder than they do so they can retire young and enjoy the things that the world has to offer.

This doesn't mean to imply that there is anything wrong with a salary or with working hard. The point is that to be wealthy you have to learn to work smarter – not harder – by creating a direct link between your compensation (notice I didn't say salary) and your results: stock options, a share of the profits, a commission on gross sales, etc.

If the solution is so simple, why don't more people do it and get wealthy that much faster? The reason is equally simple: To work for results rather than a steady paycheck requires immense courage and a strong belief in yourself. It requires a determination to go against the popular notion that a steady paycheck is the ultimate goal. It calls for more energy and time than most people want to invest.

It takes us back to the attitude of abundance, which flies in the face of every principle we ever learned. When we decide to leave the safety of the steady paycheck and go for results, we are putting our faith in the Universal Laws and our ability to succeed.

Remuneration – Not Salary

Tom entered the car business as a salesman when he was 22. For the first year, the going was rough and he had to learn on the job.

As sales grew, he learned to sell at a higher profit (adding more value to his services) and his commissions grew.

A few years later, he moved to a bigger dealership and began earning a six-figure income. He was given a car too!

Tom's plan is to become General Manager at the ripe old age of 32 – just ten years after he started.

Wealthy people know that to make it in the big league you have to be willing to invest in yourself. If you put a ceiling on your potential, that is where you will stop.

The success model becomes even easier if you can organize your business to run without your active involvement.

There's no magic formula that creates large profits from products like books, royalties from music, real estate, Internet businesses and manufacturing. It's all about leveraging your money and your time.

There is no ideal situation or job that will guarantee success. Each one of us brings a unique perspective and talent to the business of working and living our lives.

In our quest for happiness and joy, we often forget to simply let life take us where it pleases. The true measure of a successful person is his ability to go with the flow and adapt accordingly.

No one can make a foolproof plan. For all our preparations and planning, events have a tendency to unfold at their own speed. Our goal may be reached sooner or later than we expect; the situation may render the plan obsolete and oblige us to adapt or be left behind.

The secret of success lies in embracing life – not with caution and fear – but with joy and positive expectations.

In Part III we will introduce the mechanics of money and the most effective methods to make your money work for you. You will find guides and other tools to help you organize your life.

For the teenager in search of wealth, these tools and guides offer invaluable support at the starting point of success.

For the mentor, or the parent teaching their teen and learning themselves, there can be no better gift than the shared appreciation of the wealth that life has to offer.

PART THREE:

Applying the Wisdom

The Wisdom of Wealth

Each one of us would like to believe we are wise with money. Before you tell anyone that you have all the wisdom of wealth you need, let's start with a few exercises.

Teens:

Write down everything you would buy if you had all the money in the world. Don't hold yourself back. List everything, no limits.

- ....
- ....
- ....
- ....
- ....
- ....
- ....
- ....
- ....
- ....
- ....
- ....
- ....

Mentors, write your wish list on this page.

Don't hold back, list everything you would like to have, no limits if you had all the money in the world.

- ....
- ....
- ....
- ....
- ....
- ....
- ....
- ....
- ....
- ....
- ....
- ....
- ....
- ....
- ....
- ....
- ....
- ....

What Is Net Worth?

Net worth is the sum total of your assets, investments and savings – minus all your debt. It can be positive, if what you have is more than what you owe, or negative if what you owe is more than what you have.

Net worth is made up of:

- Income streams (passive income from one or more sources, and income from your work)
- Savings, either at a bank or in a company retirement account and so on
- Investments
- Assets, physical things, like a home you own outright, or a car that is fully paid off

Let's assume you earn $60,000 a year. You pay the mortgage on your home and cars; you buy the groceries and pay all the other bills. You also spend money on yourself. At the end of the month, the outstanding balance on your credit cards is in the thousands. You either pay it off in full or you make a minimum payment *and* pay interest on the complete balance that was outstanding.

Yes! You read those underlined words correctly. If your balance was $3,500 and you paid $2,000 you will still pay interest on the total amount of $3,500. (The rate of interest varies depending on the card you have and the country you live in, so call your card company and ask them for your own card's terms and conditions.)

Let's get back your income. You are hypothetically earning $60,000 a year. This figure may go up when you get a raise or a better job. This income is known as "working income", so defined because you get up in the morning, go to work, spend your whole day working, get back home at night and at the end of the month, you get paid the value of your services. You personally work for this income.

Now we come to the crucial question:

> How much do you have left over after you've finished paying for things you wanted or needed?

$100, $200, $500, maybe more? Maybe you have a hefty savings balance, some other investments, RRSP's, 401(K) and so on.

> To help you figure out where your working income is going, a budget helps you break down your expenses into **needs** versus **wants**.

What a Budget Looks Like

Income I have each month:

$5,000 net salary
$1,200

Expenses I have each month:

Rent/mortgage =

Food (restaurant; groceries) = $500
Transportation (car payment, insurance, fuel, maintenance, parking, etc. = $450
[You fill in the rest yourself!]

TOTAL:

TOTAL:

Then, add things up. Remember: If you paid for an item via credit card, you still spent the money! Write it down.

One more word on your budget. Some households or individuals self-limit and create a budget in advance. In other words, they budget in advance only $400 on food from any source – and *they do not spend more than that in any month.* That is another budgeting approach.

If you are like most people brought up in today's 'spend first, think later' world, it's unlikely that you have funds beyond your working or earned income. Take a minute to go through your budget. How much of your money is actually going toward necessities like housing, food and utilities? How much are you spending on 'impulse' items, like the cute shoes, or that new phone, you thought you couldn't live without?

Many people use shopping to ease their frustrations. The power of being able to spend what they want, where they want, when they want isn't about buying something because they need it, but rather to fill some emotional void.

Ask yourself and then ask your teen these questions.

Mentors

- Is money important to your happiness?

- Do you shop when you're sad, upset, depressed or plain bored?

- Will money get you everything you want?

- If you had more money, would that change the way you thought of yourself?

- Would other people think better of you if you had more money?

Teens

- Is money important to my happiness?

- Do I shop when I am sad, upset, depressed or plain bored?

- Will money get me everything I want?

- If I had more money, would it change the way I thought of myself?

- Would other people think better of me if I had more money?

Now let's analyze these seemingly simple questions:

Is Money Important to Your Happiness?

Most of us answer 'Yes'. Money pays the bills, buys our necessities and so on. But this question refers to money in a different way.

<u>Mentors</u>

Assume your necessities were taken care of – is money still important to your happiness?

<u>Teens</u>

Assume your necessities were taken care of – is money still important to your happiness?

Some will answer 'Yes' and others 'No'. Money is important as a tool to get you where you are going and as a reward for doing things well. But real happiness comes from within, from your thoughts and feelings of self-worth, from your image of yourself and the dreams you have that take you where you want to go.

Do you shop when you're sad, upset, depressed or plain bored?

Do you use shopping as a means to feel better about yourself? If your answer is 'Yes', it's time to sit down with those closest to you and discuss how and why you shop. Do you go shopping for the reasons listed above or other reasons you haven't discovered till now?

When you become aware of your behavior, you can begin to change. Once you know the reasons for your actions, you can tell yourself,
"Ok. I know I want to go to the mall to shop or to buy this specific item, but will it really change anything or solve any problems I have? Let me go to a quiet place and write down what is troubling me."

Anita loves to shop. She's always talking about the money she saves instead of the money she spends. She's always saying, *"I saved so much, I bought this on sale at 35% off! I saved xx dollars."*

The strangest thing is that she really believes it. She never sees the money she spends; she sees the money she saved. She has never understood that shopping her problems away doesn't work. Today she has closets full of clothes she never wears. She's still saying, *"Guess what? There was this great sale and I saved..."*

There's nothing wrong with being thrifty. A penny saved is 1.25 pennies earned (the penny you save is after-tax earnings). The important thing is to be sure you're saving on items you really need.

Try to ask yourself before each purchase whether or not you really need this item. Before you buy that piece of clothing, ask yourself why you are buying it. Is it because you need it, or is it because you *think* you need it? How will you pay for them next month if you use your credit card? Will you pay off your card in full, or will that clothing end up costing twice as much thanks to the interest you will pay?

Try the *Test of Time* Method

Try putting off whatever you desperately want at that moment – for a few hours, a day and then a week. Go back after that time is over and check out the item again. Is it still as exciting or only okay now that the impulse is gone? Do you still need it? If your answer is 'Yes', go right ahead. If 'No', walk away.

Try playing a psychological game with yourself, like this: "I *am* going to buy item X. I give myself full permission to buy it – only not right now. I'll buy it after a few _____ (hours, a few days ... fill in this blank)."

This trains you to accept deferred pleasures (a wealthy person's secret). You will enjoy much greater satisfaction when you do buy and you will end up saving money that you might otherwise have spent impulsively on things you just thought you wanted. Put that saved money to work for you and watch your wealth grow.

Will Money Get You Everything You Want?

Yes, if your goals are based on your strengths and your talent. No, if you chase money for the wrong reasons.

For example, if you managed to win the lottery or inherited lots of money, but aren't happy with the person you are or the choices you have made, the money won't get you what you want. If, on the other hand, you always worked at something that gave you satisfaction over and above the money it earned, then the windfall money would enable you to live your life to its full potential in every way.

It's essential that you discuss the reasons behind your career options (mentor and teen) before you set yourself up for failure or a lifetime spent chasing happiness through money. As the wealthy know, money comes to those who value and delight in it; to those who work at something because they enjoy it for the rewards inherent in the work – beyond the money it brings.

Would More Money Change the Way You Think of Your Inner Self?

If your answer is 'yes, money will make me happy,' you need to analyze your need for approval. Each and every one of us comes into this world complete in and of ourselves. We meet dozens of people in one day but we don't necessarily remember them all or approve of them all. To be truly successful, it is essential to be true to yourself. If you are true to yourself, money will not change your opinion about the inner you.

Ask yourself this question: Would other people think better of you if you had more money? If the answer is 'Yes!' you are keeping the wrong company! It might be time to take a closer look at your friends.

To be wealthy you have to think beyond your working income, beyond what you earn as a salary today and in the future.

You can never grow wealthy if you spend every cent you make to live. To grow wealthy, you have to start making your money work for you. Think in terms of net worth.

Think long-term versus short-term. Think assets that go up in value versus expenses that are here to stay.

Passive Income

We've already discussed "working" income – the money you earn in exchange for the work you do. Passive income is income that comes to you without having to spend energy to earn it. In other words, you generally do not have to work at it *daily* as you would at a job, to get passive income. You do the "work" once, and it pays you over and over.

Examples include residual earnings and royalty sales from books or music you have written, or an invention of yours; an online business (YouTube video production, or affiliate sales) can bring you advertising or commission income. Other sources of passive income can be generated from properties you own and rent out like apartment buildings or commercial space, etc.

To be wealthy you have to think beyond working income, beyond what you earn as a salary today and in the future. To be wealthy you have to start thinking in terms of your accumulated net worth. Think long-term versus short-term! Assets that go up in value versus expenses that are here to stay.

What Net Worth Looks Like

In a budget labels are "income and expenses", and "assets and liabilities".

You can add up your assets, including the value of your house, any cars that you own, any investments, checking and saving accounts and the value of any other savings/investment plans that you might have.

When you put down the value of your house or your vehicle in the assets column, put in the complete value you think you'd get if it were to be sold today.

Then in the liability column, list, value and total up the amount you owe on it in terms of mortgage principal, car payments remaining, credit card balances due, loans still outstanding, etc.

Subtract the total liabilities from the total assets. This is your net worth.

We have looked at how to create a budget and how to calculate net worth. Let's do some exercises with both concepts now.

Your Current Budget

Go through the credit card statements for the last few months or receipts if you use cash or banks statements if you use debit cards and fill in the amounts.

How much did you spend on food and other necessities?

_____

How much on needs and how much on wants?

_____

How much on impulse shopping because there was a 'sale' on?

_____

Did you plan to buy the things you bought or did it just happen?

_____

Do you have money left over at the end of the month?

_____

Have you maxed out your credit?

_____

Do you pay a fee every time you withdraw cash from a bank machine, and if so, how much?

_____

Now assign yourself a certain sum of money and make a budget of what you will or will not buy, based on the list you made at the start of this book.

Budget for Mentors & Parents

Now assign your teens a certain sum of money and ask them to make a budget of what they will or will not buy, based on the list they made at the start of this book.

Budget for Teens

Ask your teen to list what they think their net worth is here. What do they own that is of value?

Have your teen go over this list when they complete this book. Ask them to judge for themselves what things are of value, based on the knowledge they have gained.

Let's assume that you are not a teen any more. You're grown up and you have a job. This job gets you $2,000 in take home pay monthly.

What would your budget look like, or to be more precise, how would your monthly expense statement look?

Let's assume you aren't staying at home:

First let's chop off taxes, at the rate of 20%. That is $400.

So now you have $1,600 left. The apartment rent is $700.

Now you have $900 left. You spend $400 on the car (all included), $220 on other expenses (phone, hydro, cell phone etc.) and $120 on groceries for yourself. You have about $80 left and there is still clothing to buy, eating out, shopping and having fun left.

Where did all the money go???

It's difficult to make your dollars stretch when an emergency comes up and you are strapped for cash. Even if your salary were to go up slightly, you would still run short of cash because your spending would increase accordingly. It's just human nature.

Managing your Money

Now that you know how much you have and understand what a budget is, this brings us to money *management.*

Sounds like the simplest thing on earth! After all, everyone knows that to be wealthy you have to manage your money. Everyone knows, but do they do it? No! Do you?

When asked, almost everyone replies, "Well, if I *had* money, I would manage it, wouldn't I!" We mistakenly believe that only people with huge amounts of money need to worry about managing it.

Those who wait to have money before they manage it have already limited their potential because waiting – not managing – is what they are training themselves to do!

Imagine a gardener saying, "I have a few seeds but I can't plant them or make them grow until I have a whole lot of them." Instead of waiting for the 'whole lot' to arrive, he could have planted the seeds he had and be enjoying their fruit by now.

The secret of wealth is this: once you start managing whatever money you have, more of it will manage to find its way to you.

Mentors, now is a good time to go over the budget and the net worth subjects with your teens. What would you do differently? What would you buy or not buy?

See how they stand on Spending versus Brands and Necessities versus Needs. For example, a computer may be a desire for someone, but a need for another. Similarly, an artist would need art supplies, yet the same items could be a luxury for another person. One person can make do with a single basic handbag and the other feels incomplete without color-coordinated brand name accessories.

Where does each of you stand? What needs to be changed?

Are you happy as you are – or do you think you can prune your spending in a particular category (i.e.: eating out less often, etc.)?

What would you do with the money you saved?
Would you spend it, save it or invest it?

Once you set yourself up to think in these terms (spend, save or invest) you are on your way to developing the mindset that will enable you to fulfill your ⓔ *Potential.*

To Have Money, You Have to Manage It

The types of questions we just asked lead you to making money management decisions.

Unless you start by managing what you have, it will never grow into more and you will never have enough money to manage.

Whether you have one dollar as a child, 50 dollars as a teen or a couple of thousand dollars as an adult, you have to learn to manage it. Why? Because our expenses have a bad habit of growing as our income grows.

Think back: How much did you earn as a child, a teen and a young adult? What were your expenses? As your income or allowance increased, didn't your expenses increase, too? So many 'wants' suddenly became 'needs' you simply had to acquire with your newfound disposable income!

Unless we learn to manage our money, it will manage us. It will own us in the form of bills, outstanding payments, debts or worse.

Managing money is your excuse to focus on and pay daily attention to the business of getting wealthy. When you manage money, more comes to you. It flies in with greater speed and in bigger amounts than ever before. No matter what the amount, start managing it and watch your *Money Baskets* begin to grow... Part IV of the book has complete details on the 5 different *Money Baskets* you need to set up and how to go about doing it, so stay the course.

To start managing it, you first and foremost deduct 10% at source and put it away in a separate savings account or in a piggy bank (sounds funny, but it actually works).

To be successful you must put away the 10% *before* you take a single penny from your money. Whether you got that money as a gift, a salary, part of an allowance or whatever, take out 10% and put it away first. Immediately, you will feel a sense of control and power over your money and you will be amazed at how quickly that feeling will grow.

Putting your Money to Work

There is no point in having money unless you *make* it work for you.

Money just sitting in the bank in a current account will remain virtually stagnant and achieve nothing unless you put it to work.

Let's take the case of Peter, who had worked hard for a number of years and saved his money. In time, he moved on to greener pastures and settled down comfortably. He put half of all his saved cash in the bank, and used the other half to reward himself for his hard work. Peter spent half of his saved money building an extravagant new life.

But it took Peter longer than he expected to find a new job. As time went by, he continued to dip into his savings, using the capital to support his lavish lifestyle. In just one year, his savings were gone. Peter was desperate. He had to give up his extravagant ways and go back to his old job!

We have all read stories of how wealthy people suddenly become poor. The main reason this happens is because they failed to put their money to work for them. The financial expert says that the money you save is called your "principal". You never, ever spend your principal (which is what Peter did). You only spend the "interest", or new money, that it earns for you (which Peter did not do).

Unless you invest the extra money that you have, it will not grow and earn interest for you. The more it grows and earns for you, the more you will have and the more you can use to support new growth. Money begets money ... but you have to know how to put it to work. Once you have a small Money Basket, discuss your options with your parents, mentors or financial advisors and choose the safest and most profitable way of putting your money to work. Safety first means you are protecting the principal as best you can. If something sounds too good to be true, don't go for it, as it might be risky.

Teens – let's continue the previous exercise:

Let's assume you are earning $2,000 every month and after tax you get $1,600. What would happen if you were to put away 10% of your money before doing anything else? In effect, you would be paying yourself before you paid anyone else.

$160 would be $1,920 saved in one year. In 5 years, assuming your salary didn't go up, you would have $9,600 saved. If you were to put that money to work in the form of a safe investment and it earned money every month, it would set you on the path to future wealth.

Now you invest this money in something safe and lucrative. After all, you don't want your hard-won savings to be put to risk and lost in some hare-brained scheme.

So be cautious in your investments, ask for good advice, get 2nd and 3rd opinions and constantly seek to expand your knowledge.

Wealthy people have enough money put away in investments (passive income from interest) that support them so they don't need to work unless they want to.

Example:

A wealthy person who has accumulated $2,000,000 in principal might invest it all at 4% cumulative annual interest (he gets an extra 4% on the money each year).

This means he gets $80,000 at the end of the first year in interest – 4% of his $2M. The second year his principal amount earning interest has grown to $2M + $80,000 or *$2,080,000.* He gets an extra $83,200 at the end of year two, as 4% interest on $2,080,000 is $83,200. If he spends nothing, but adds that to his $2,080,000, he earns even more interest in year three, because his new principal is *$2,163,200.* And on and on, year after year. WOW!

It is cumulative and thus grows ever faster each year.

They can choose to spend that interest (for instance, using it all for his living expenses) or reinvest it because he doesn't need it yet.

That should be your aim, too: to live your life the way you want to, free of financial pressures. You can achieve this goal when your passive income is greater than your living expenses. If the wealthy person in the example above only needed $50,000 per year, he'd be living "within his means."

To take the first step in that direction, you need a few tips on breaking the money barrier. Let's look at eleven rules of wealth.

Rule #1: There are no rules when it comes to talking about money. Talk about money with your friends, your parents and your guardians, whoever will respond to your conversational gambits.

The more you talk, the more you will be exposed to different ideas and viewpoints and the more your thinking will evolve. Pretty soon, you could be the one – the financial guru -- everyone looks to for guidance.

Rule #2: When you pull out your wallet, or debit card, stop and ask yourself, do you need what you are buying or is it because money gives you a feeling of power and increases your feelings of well-being?

Rule #3: If you aren't the type to fill in complicated charts and generally work yourself into a sweat over money, then opt for a simple Excel spreadsheet. Something is better than nothing, and once you start, maybe the sheer pleasure of seeing your money grow will have you filling out all sorts of charts with all the dedication of a certified accountant.

Rule #4: Save some of the money you get. 10% is ideal. Don't touch that money unless you intend to grow it into more money.

Rule #5: Don't be desperate to buy stuff. Think of options. It's very cool today "to simplify one's life" and to "downsize." Maybe you can do that. Alternatively, maybe there is a T-shirt you can paint over because it looks dull instead of buying a new one for $20. Stick embroidered patches on your jeans. Shop at second-hand stores. This is called "repurposing" and is also very trendy now.

An entry from *Carly's Diary* says this:

> *"Sometimes I so desperately want to buy something. One time it was a Tamagotchi and it was a real craving. But somehow, I held on for a week and then suddenly the craving passed and I didn't want the Tamagotchi anymore. Now I'd rather have an mp3*

*player... I get influenced really easily, but because I
know I get influenced, I try to hold on to see if I want
something because I really want it or I want it
because I think I do."*

Rule #6: Most people learn by mistakes and you will, too.
Experimenting with small sums of money earlier in life is
better than doing it when you are grown up and thousands
of dollars are at stake.

Rule #7: Set your goals and ask your
parents/guardian/aunt/uncle to help you reach them. They
just might be a goldmine of recommendations!

Rule #8: No matter how great the temptation, don't ask
for a credit or debit card. Deal with real cash until you learn
the real value of money. It is too easy to get carried away
with a piece of plastic and get trapped under a mountain of
debt. When it is time to get used to using a credit card,
start with a small amount and pay it off in FULL every
month.

Rule #9: Read this book again and again. Each time you
read it, you will get more value from it.

Rule #10: Follow your heart. This is by far the most
important rule. If something feels wrong, don't do it – no
matter what peer pressure is telling you! And if something

feels right, take the risk and go for it... each of us has the seed of genius within us, if we would only listen!

Rule #11: Make your own *Wealthy Teen Club* and learn from each other. Then in turn you could teach younger kids some money sense.

Earning Money

Here are some ways you can earn money, starting with the obvious taken-for-granted ways:

- **Babysitting services:** A great one if you are good with kids. Make sure you have done a government-sponsored babysitting course and that you are well trained in what to do, especially in case of emergencies. Check out all the rules and regulations and be very thorough before you take on the responsibility of looking after a young person. Be sure to have your parents or mentors meet the people you will be working for.

In addition to the ever-popular babysitting:

- **Allowance:** Approach you parents about this. If you are not old enough to have a job, this will give you some money to manage on your own. It is important to start to hold money, to decide how to save and spend it wisely.

- **Do extra chores:** You can do this for friends, family or neighbors. You might take up dog-walking, plant-care, window-washing, car washing or painting someone's door (window trim, etc.) for them. If you are great in the kitchen, offer to cook a special meal for a small fee (over and above the food costs). Offer to do chores in return for some kind of cash payment and make it a point to mention that you are saving your money (or at least part of it). Our grand-mothers called it their "Egg money" – the cash they got selling their hens' surplus eggs – literally!

- **Have a garage sale**: Organize a garage sale and make some money off your old rejects. Who knows, you might become the neighborhood expert on garage sales. Similarly, you could have a bake sale to raise money for a specific purpose.

- **Try out a job**: If you can't do a job through the school year, get set up to have a job in the summer. The possibilities are endless and limited only to what you want to do and what is legally possible. Make sure you check out everything (safety issues and whether you are allowed to do it) before taking a summer job.

- **Making movies or taking photos**: For a tech savvy teen, it's no hardship to be the official photographer or videographer at a family function – a friend's wedding or a parent's anniversary party. If you are really good, hire yourself to do parties. What's more, today's DVD players and computers with CD burners make it a snap to create short films. It's a great way to put your expensive toys to work for you. Make sure where you are going is safe and that an adult knows where you are at all times.

- **Design something to sell**: Teenager Madison Robinson from Texas, launched her flip-flop business when she was 13. She had come up with this idea when she was eight. She is now a millionaire!

- **Car washing**: Adults love having their car clean inside and out without having to wash it themselves – or drive down to a car wash. If you like the idea, make up a few flyers and test it within the neighborhood first. Of course, your first customer could be your mentor!

- **Computer servicing**: Another great job for tech-savvy teens helps people who know how to use a computer but couldn't fix one to save their lives. A word of caution: make sure you know what you are doing – you don't want to end up being liable for an expensive piece of equipment.

- **Computer tutor**: Many people who own computers don't know the basics of accessing the Internet, using basic word processing or calculation software and other functions young people today take for granted. You could offer to run classes. Be sure to check with your mentors to decide on a good place. There should be other adults around (preferably your mentor/ parent/ guardian) for your safety. You could work out lesson plans and charge for 5 lessons at a time, for instance.

- **Online auctions** or classifieds: Carly's Diary gives an insight into the great idea she thought up. Why not set up your own online 'money-making' business? It requires a big idea, a little money and a lot of hard work. Interested? We read about numerous teens today earning serious money from helpful YouTube videos and other online options.

- **Pool cleaning**: This one would depend on the number of pools in your neighborhood, so do the research before you set yourself up in business.

- **Lawn maintenance**: Seniors who can't move around very well anymore still love a well-manicured yard and garden. From offering a basic grass-cutting service or a raking leaves service, you could get into garden landscaping with vegetables, plants and flowers. Sure it's hard, sweaty work, but if you love to be outdoors, have a green thumb and a good sense of natural beauty, you could "rake" in good money over a few short spring and summer months.

- **Garbage/rubbish service**: Again, some seniors in your neighborhood may find it difficult to do this chore. They may be happy to contract their rubbish needs to you! You could haul out the rubbish bins for pickup and then put them away again.

Easy Tips on Saving

- Once you have money coming in, save at least 10% of it (read Carly's Diary to see how she saved up almost $1500).

- You could also ask your parents to help you save by matching dollar to dollar (on what you save).

- Before you buy something, stop and think if this dollar would do better working for you somewhere else.

- Spend just what you need.

- Save what you were going to spend JLT (Just Like That) and set that money to work earning money for you.

This book isn't telling you to be cheap, stingy or miserly. The idea is to know where you are spending and why before you spend. Don't spend wildly. Track your wealth. You can have fun and be practical too. In other words, create balance in your spending habits.

Carly's Diary suggests keeping 10% aside for savings and 10% for FUN! Yes: FUN!

For other ideas on how to save money and have fun too, you'll have to read **Carly's Diary**. In the meantime read on to see what some of our *Wealthy Teen* members are telling us about their spending and saving routines.

Here's what some teens are saying

- I keep very little money in my pocket. Just enough to get by and another $10 for emergencies. I know if I have money I'll spend it. – D. B. (15)

- I spend the dollars and keep all the change one month, from the amount I have allotted myself. Then another month, I will spend only the change and keep the dollars aside. I am in competition with myself to see how much I can save ... it's like a game and it's fun too. – R. C. (16)

- I love to hoard money. Every time I get some, I stash it away in the bank and gloat over my growing pile. Someday I plan on being mega wealthy. – A. B. (12)

- I wait to see if I really want the something I want to buy, or it's just the ads on TV talking. – M. L. (13)

- I put away my savings in another account so I don't see them. What I can't see, I don't miss. – L. R. (15)

Teens: What ideas do you have? Write them down here:

_____

_____

_____

_____

_____

_____

Mentors: Do you have any ideas? If so list them here:

_____

_____

_____

_____

_____

_____

Are you spending more than you should? Do you need to balance your budget? Write down the amount of money you have, the amount of money you are spending currently, and changes you need to make.

If you find the whole thing overwhelming at the moment, remember that you can always start with the income/expense sheet, which is the simplest one. When you're ready, you can move on to weekly accounts and finally start keeping track of your money on a daily basis.

Before you know it, it will become as automatic a habit as checking your email and soon you won't be able to sleep at night unless you have your accounts balanced. If and when that happens, you can be sure you are on your way to wealth and even greater satisfaction. When you control your money, your money doesn't control you or your life!!

P.S. Ask yourself this question:

"If I am a wealthy teenager today, what kind of a man or woman will I be, when I am grown up?"

Answer: Even Wealthier!

PART FOUR:

Building Your Money Baskets

Building Your Financial Baskets

Hi! It's Carly again.

So, what did you think of all those lessons? Did it make sense to you that some of your friends are dragging you down with their negative 'whatever' talk instead of having anything to say? Did those 'where do you think you're going' poor crabs remind you of anyone? I thought it was totally cool that the box with the wealthy crabs was always empty. And what did you think of the girl making all that money just by teaching swimming classes in her family's pool, or by designing flip flops? Was that amazing?

There are so many great ideas out there just waiting for us to make them happen that it makes me shake my head when I hear my friends say there's nothing to do but go to the mall because they're so totally bored.

It suddenly hit me that they've given up on the best part of being a teen. I mean, right now is an amazing time for us to get started building our dreams: we're full of such great ideas, we have all these teachers and school resources to go to for help and support when we need them and we have our parents looking after all the seriously expensive responsibilities that are going to take up a major part of our time and attention later on.

I don't spend as much time with the bored kids as I used to.

When you see so much opportunity everywhere, how can anyone say things are unfair? Why would you float through school in a fog and then stay out all night with a bunch of strangers who don't have any dreams? I love to party, but not until I've got something worth celebrating: something I've worked hard for that really means something to me. How can you have a party and dance and go crazy if you haven't done anything? What kind of sense does that make?

I feel really sorry for the kids who hit their teens and expect someone to hand everything to them on a plate. They act like Life is this big screen TV somebody put there in front of them and they're waiting for a better show to come on. They're not even willing to reach for the remote: they just sit there and complain. About the only thing they make any effort to do is talk about the stuff they'll buy when they get to the mall.

I told my Mom that I didn't get any of it and she said, 'Maybe they're not ready to take the next steps, honey. Maybe they're afraid of change, like the poor crabs, and they're looking for ways to put off the decision to go forward. Maybe the negativity makes them feel safe.'

I think she's right. And that's why I think this book is the best idea we ever had. It's perfectly normal to be afraid that a new idea won't work exactly as you planned. But you'll never know if it will fail or succeed until you give it a try!

This section of the book is a step-by-step outline that will help you understand how to start managing your money so you can have the power to give all those great new ideas of yours a chance.

See ya!

Back to Lorna:

Carly is absolutely right. You have to believe in yourself and open your mind to opportunity in order to succeed at anything. While you're doing that, you also have to make a plan that will support you and your dreams as you move ahead.

To be successful, to be wealthy and to maximize your ⓔ Potential, it is essential to understand, appreciate and apply the principle of the 5 *Baskets*. This is very cool, since most people don't consider more than one basket for themselves.

The line below represents your income for a month, after tax

A_____B

INCOME

To fill the baskets that will support you, you need to take that monthly income amount and divide it by the percentages you see listed in the five categories below. Each category is a basket.

A__	10%__	10%__	10%__	20%__	50%__	__B
	Savings Basket	*Fun Basket*	*Charity Basket*	*Investment Basket*	*Essentials Basket*	

You need to get in the habit of looking at any money that comes in as naturally falling into these five baskets. Instead of saying, 'I make $1,600 a month after taxes', you need to say, 'I have $160 saved for a rainy day, $160 for fun just for me, $160 to help others less fortunate, $320 to invest in the future and $800 to pay all my bills'.

When you begin to see your money slotted into in those five separate baskets, it becomes much easier to limit your impulse spending and stay within your budget. You are less likely to 'borrow' from one basket to support an indulgence in another.

---

5 Baskets = Your Total Income

Savings + Fun + Charity + Investments + Essentials = Total Income

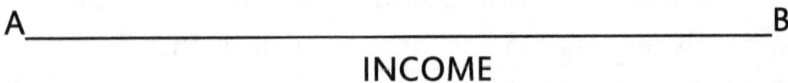

A_____B

INCOME

The only reason it seems strange to think of your money in separate baskets like this is because you've never done it before. It's going to continue to seem strange until this new habit becomes automatic and replaces the old habit you had before of just lumping everything into one big pile and crossing your fingers to make things work out right all the time.

People will tell you that it takes 30 days to create a habit. That's perfect! That gives you a month to organize everything and make your first mistakes before your next $1,600 comes along and you're ready to take charge.

If you follow this plan, it will help you achieve your ⓔ **Potential** *and maximize your earnings in life.* Now it's time to learn all about *The Money Baskets.*

The Savings Basket

The Art of Paying Yourself First

The Savings **Basket** represents 10% of your total income after tax. In the earlier exercise we created for teens, 10% of the income after tax amounted to over $9000 over a period of 5 years. We'll show it to you again, to make sure it's clear:

We have assumed that you are earning $2,000 every month and after tax you get $1,600. If you were to put away 10% of your money before doing anything else, you would be paying yourself <u>before</u> you paid anyone else. That is your Savings Basket.

With an after-tax income of $1,600 coming in every month, 10% is $160. Multiply that $160 by 12 months and you get $1,920 in a year. In 5 years, assuming your salary didn't change, you would have $1920 x 5, or $9600 saved.

And that is without calculating interest, compound interest or any other benefit the money could have earned if it had been put to work.

The first rule of growing rich? Pay yourself first!

All the experts are unanimous on this point. Paying yourself first means putting away 10% of your income into a separate savings account (or glass jar, or whatever you use) before you use a penny of it to pay a bill or spend on something.

When you take that money out at the beginning, four things happen:

1. You won't notice the money that is missing.
2. Your spending habits will shift to accommodate the slightly smaller balance in your account.
3. Your savings account will grow quickly without you realizing it.
4. Saving money attracts money and for that reason alone, your income will increase.

It's hard to believe till you try it for yourself, but it actually works!

So the Savings Basket will be made up of the 10% that you put aside to pay yourself first, no matter how much or how little money you get or whatever its source.

This means that the rule applies to *every source of money income*, not just the money you get from your job. If someone gives you a check on your birthday, if you sell some stuff at a garage sale, or if your parents give you an allowance ... wherever the money comes from, the 10% rule applies. As soon as you get the money, 10% goes into your Savings Basket to pay yourself.

Look at this:

Suppose you got $5 from your Aunt and Uncle on your birthday and your grandmother gave you $20. Your Mom and Dad matched that with $25 of their own. That's $50. Right away, you put $5 into your Savings Basket.

On Saturday, you and your family have a garage sale. Your share comes to $60. Your Savings Basket gets another $6.

You get your weekly allowance on Wednesdays. It's $20. You put $2 in your Savings Basket. In four weeks you put in $8 altogether.

The neighbor across the street fell and broke her hip. She hires you to run errands for her every day for a month. She gives you a crisp $10 bill every day after you're done. Every night, $1 goes into your Savings Basket. At the end of the month, $31 more have found their way into that Basket.

You add up your savings: $5 + $6 + $8 + 31 = $50

You're probably thinking that if you just kept all the money together, you'd really have $500 to spend right now. Wow! But the purpose of this exercise is to show you how to work with a little bit less now so that you can have a lot more than $500 in the future.

By saving 10% first, regardless of the amount, you are training your mind to pay yourself first. Once this concept takes hold and you see your money begin to grow, you will value yourself even more as an individual worthy of the good things in life. So even if you have got only $20, put away $2 in your savings account.

Bonus Rewards

- Your new habit is reinforced
- You save money
- You'll feel good about having saved

If you are a mentor with a fixed salary, you could arrange to have it deducted automatically from your checking account and transferred to a savings account. You won't even see the money and it will continue to add up.

Putting 10% away in a savings account is the time-tested foundation of realizing your ⓔ *Potential* and creating wealth. So begin it today.

A__   10%__
       Savings
       Basket

What should you do once you have started saving and have
a small amount of cash in your account?

We'll come to that in the Investment Basket, but for now
let's move on to the Fun Basket.

The Fun Basket

The Art of Enjoying Life

You have to have fun! To maintain the balance that is essential in Life, you have to budget your time and your money to allow yourself to play as a reward for working hard. Building a Fun Basket to treat yourself and generally enjoy life is a big priority if you hope to be a success.

In a lot of ways, managing your money is a lot like managing your diet. If you eat nothing but simple, low-calorie meals all the time, you will get fed up with the rigid routine. When you rebel and eat all the things you've forbidden yourself to have, you gain back all the weight you worked so hard to lose.

To win over the long term, there must be balance. To balance the 10% Savings Basket, there must be an equal 10% Fun Basket, too.

From the money that you earned, you have already put away 10% in your Savings Basket to pay yourself first. That leaves you with 90%. You will put away another 10% from that balance remaining in your Fun Basket. You must spend it on things that you desire (not need) and on impulse purchases.

Going back to our example with the Savings Basket, if you have been able to put away $50 to pay yourself first, you can also put $50 away for Fun – to reward yourself for working hard. Every step you are taking is for you. Isn't this great??? You can use the Fun Basket money any time you want because you are in control.

A__   10%___   10%___
        Savings   Fun
        Basket   Basket

The Charity Basket

The Art of Giving

You're beginning to notice that the success formula is all about balance: work and play, save and spend, take and give. That's because Life itself is a balanced equation. Working against nature is like trying to walk up the 'down' escalator: you have to work twice as hard just to stay in one place.

We've shown you how to pay yourself first with your Savings Basket and then reward yourself with your Fun Basket. Now it's time to balance the equation and give something back. It's time to put money into your Charity Basket so it goes back in circulation to work for other people as it works for you.

With 10% in your Savings Basket and 10% in your Fun Basket, you have 80% of your income after taxes left. Choose the charity or cause that is closest to your heart to donate the next 10%.

You may find it difficult to put aside 10% at first. When Carly set up her Money Baskets, she didn't have enough room in her budget to donate that much right away. She chose to give 5% and donate her time as a volunteer to make up the rest.

Something you will have noticed about yourself, and other people too, is that you always mean to do everything on this list. The problem is in actually getting around to it. That's because Life keeps grabbing our attention and getting in the way.

We have created this simple system of breaking your money into these categories automatically, so that you don't even have to think about it once the habit takes hold. Every time you get money, you will automatically divide it up as we are showing you. Why? Because you're beginning to realize that this method really works!

Automatically giving 10% to pay yourself, reward yourself and help others will become second-nature to you before you know it.

As a mentor, you might already be doing something like this on a less formal basis. If you aren't, now is a great time to make it a regular part of your life.

The act of giving keeps you focused on your place in the world. You experience a totally new kind of pleasure when you help someone in need and the skills and knowledge you gain in the process are worth far more than the dollar value of the money itself. Giving balances God's world. Gifts return to you ten-fold.

A____   10%____   10%____   10%____
         Savings   Fun   Charity
         Basket   Basket   Basket

Going back to our example in which you had managed to
accumulate $500 at the end of the month, you have put
aside $50 for Savings and $50 for Fun. Now you are going
to put aside $50 for Charity. This makes a grand total of
$150, or 30% of your money. Let's see what we can do with
the remaining 70%.

The Investment Basket

The Art of Making Money Work

You're a busy person, aren't you! You're going to school and working hard to complete your assignments and keep up your grades. You probably take part in an organized sport. Maybe you belong to a special interest group or club that meets after school. In addition to the chores you do at home, you may have a part-time job. You like to spend time with your family and you hang out with your friends whenever you can.

You've added money management to the list and a lot of new ideas and opportunities are beginning to present themselves. As you earn your money, you're automatically saving some, having fun with some and giving some to charity.

Every one of these things you are doing is focused on your life today. Now it's time to look at a portion of your income with an eye on the future.

Whether you've been adding 10% to your Savings Basket regularly or you've just begun, it won't take long before you'll find that the balance in your Savings account has grown to a sizeable sum. What you need to keep in mind as you watch your savings grow, is that you are really doing two separate things with this account.

The first thing you are doing is creating a cushion of safety for those unexpected emergencies that always seem to come along when you least expect them. You want to create a dollar figure in your mind that you call your buffer. You want to make sure that you always have at least that much in your Savings account at all times.

The second thing you are doing is looking for an opportunity to take the extra money out of your Savings account when the balance is bigger than your buffer and transfer it into your investment account.

For example, let's say that you've been building your Money Baskets long enough to have a balance in your savings account of $5,000. You have done your homework and calculated that $3,000 is a sufficient amount for emergencies. Your next step is to move the remaining balance of $2,000 ($5,000 - $3,000 = $2,000) into your investment account.

You're probably wondering what the difference is between Savings and Investment, so here is a very simple explanation:

A Savings account pays a small amount of interest on the balance you have in the bank. An Investment account puts your money to work earning more interest than the bank can offer you.

In some cases, you may use the money in your Investment account to buy something that will help you do your work better or earn more money. You might use the money in your investment account to save for something big, like a car, for instance. In that case, you might divide your investment account and put half the money toward investing and half toward saving for your future big purchase.

The purpose of an Investment Basket is to help you plan for your future, even as you manage your money today. Because the price of things goes up over time – this is called 'inflation' – you will want to put a little more in your Investment Basket, if you can.

Going back to our formula, you have 70% of your income after taxes available to you now. Take 20% of that money – or $100 according to our example – and put it into your Investment Basket.

A__	10%___	10%___	10%___	**20%___**
	Savings	Fun	Charity	Investments
	Basket	Basket	Basket	Basket

If you're not sure you can put that much into Investments yet, stay with the same 10% you have put into the other Baskets. If you do that, the chart would look like this:

A__	10%__	10%__	10%__	**10%__**
	Savings	Fun	Charity	Investments
	Basket	Basket	Basket	Basket

With those Baskets taken care of, it's time to get down to business!

The Essentials Basket

The Art of Meeting Needs

The balance of your income after taxes is now 50% or 60% of the original amount you earned, depending on the percentage you put aside for your Investment Basket. This balance is what you have to work with to meet your day-to-day needs.

If you're earning an allowance and doing odd jobs and you live at home, as we talked about before, you won't make a lot of money but you won't have a lot of expenses either. In that $500 example we created, you can probably cover your needs quite easily with $250.

If you are living on your own, earning $2,000 a month and bringing home $1,600 after taxes, this formula leaves you with either $800 or $960 to cover your expenses for the month. Can you do it? Let's go back and take another look at that example in detail.

The rent on your apartment is $700. If you got a roommate, that would cut your rent in half, so let's say it's $350. That leaves you with $450 or $510, depending on the percentage you put into your Investment Basket.

If you spend $400 on a car, you won't have anything left. Maybe you want to think about taking public transit or car-pooling for a while, just until you've saved enough to afford to operate a car. A public transit pass is roughly $100/month and the government will give you a tax credit for taking public transit. That's a great deal! Car-pooling may require you to pay a share of the fuel, but it, too, is a better deal than driving on your own.

Okay. You have $350 or $410. Your $220 for phone, heat and hydro will be split with your roommate so the bill is now $110. You have $240 or $300 left. You'll spend more on groceries with two of you, but you'll be splitting that. Let's say it's $200 divided in half, or $100.

You're left with $250 or $310. Your cell phone, health and beauty products, clothing care (laundry expenses) and work supplies are left. Divide the balance into four weekly amounts. If you can live on $60/week, you can put 20% into your Investment Basket. If you need $75/week, you'll invest 10%.

You may feel this is cutting things too close to the line. You may want to look at ways to trim the plan a little more in order to meet your needs. You can always cut the Charity Basket in half and volunteer your time. You can cut back on the Fun Basket a little as well. Make the necessary adjustments so that the equation works for you. Just remember that no matter what you do, <u>DO NOT</u> break the Savings Basket where you pay yourself first. That is the only way to build success and wealth.

Mentors, if your Essentials are much higher than the money you have available, look over your expenses carefully and see where you can save. Do you need to eat out as often or buy so much or have all the channels on TV? Try to cut a few corners where it is feasible.

Teens, your expenses will be lower if you are living at home. You might ask your parents to let you pay a nominal rent (even no rent at all) or just cover one utility bill as your contribution – for the first year, just until your Baskets are fully operational. You could leave the percentages in Fun and Investments blank and set up Baskets for special goals: hair and spa treatment, electronics needs, acting classes, education, car, trips/travel, etc.

Examples: Special Purpose Baskets

Some people we know have set up a *Christmas Basket*, so they are not caught short at holiday time for gifts and special party/meal purchases. It is a separate savings account at the bank.

We know a young man who immigrated here with his parents when he was young, and who got his first part-time cash job at age 10. Wow. You know that – in addition to his *Essentials Basket* (which he voluntarily paid over to his father for a long time) – he had one **50%** Basket? He called it the *Restaurant Basket*. He wanted to own one or more restaurants! Today, years later, he has started doing just that, and has been very successful.

Whatever you decide, get into the habit of planning before you spend, so that you make financially savvy choices. You may find yourself setting a new trend rather than doing what everyone does. If you follow the plan as outlined, your income is divided as follows:

Your Money Baskets

A_	10%___	10%___	10%___	20%___	50%	_B
	Savings Basket	Fun Basket	Charity Basket	Investments Basket	Essentials Basket	

These 5 Baskets come together to form your future. It is in your hands whether you manage your money or your money manages you.

Remember

5 Baskets = Total Income = Realizing your ⓔ Potential = Wealth

=

Wealthy Teen and Wealthy Mentor

PART FIVE:

Entrepreneurship and Your e Potential

Discovering your ⓔ *Potential* Quiz

Do you that you do really have what it takes to be successful at this?

How much are you already earning? How much more do you believe you *could* earn? Do you think you will be successful in life or do you think it will be tough going to just get by?

There are a few basic truths you must examine and take to heart if any of this information or any of these exercises are going to work for you. They have to do with understanding money, wealth and success – not as absolutes that are written in stone, but as flexible concepts that are meant to be shaped to suit you.

All of us work for money in one form or another. It is a way of exchanging services and products for other services and products that keeps our society healthy.

There is nothing wrong with having a good job. From a purely practical perspective, the money we are paid for the work we do allows us to pay our bills and live with a certain level of comfort. For those who prefer to live a simple existence, having money in the bank can be thought of as a form of insurance.

There is nothing wrong with spending the money you earn. Where people go wrong is when they spend everything and save nothing. The idea is to pay for today and prepare for tomorrow by putting a portion of your money aside.

There are many ways to save money and all of them are good as long as they suit your temperament. Stocks and investment funds may represent a higher risk than you like. Investing in land and buildings – real estate – can be rewarding for those who are willing to do the work.

Investing in a business of your own can provide financial and personal rewards, especially if it is a business are passionate about.

Persistent, consistent effort wins every time. Remember: As you believe and behave, you will become.

To help you identify your strengths and weaknesses and guide you toward your goal of wealth and success, we have designed a simple, twenty-five question test. You may want to make a second copy of the test so that your teen can try it separately. It might be fun to make several copies and let other members of your family and friends give it a try!

Answer the questions as honestly as you can without cheating and looking at the answers.

Are you ready to discover your ⓔ Potential? Let's begin!

1. What are most of our spending patterns based on?

2. "I think, therefore I am" is a simple rule to increase what?

3. When passion is combined with action and _____, true wealth can be created.

4. Events or circumstances that operate for or against an individual – that are not a direct result of their own efforts – are called what?

5. The law of tithing suggests that what percentage of your net income should be given away?

6. What one factor can keep a person motivated about their work?

7. True or False: Wealthy people avoid negativity.

8. True or False: People who become wealthy behave as if they are wealthy; they associate with wealthy people and learn from them.

9. Yes or No: Do you feel it is important to make a mark in life?

10. Yes or No: Are you prepared to take risks in life?

11. Yes or No: Do you find decision-making difficult?

12. Yes or No: I dislike negotiating / haggling over prices or other aspects of business.

13. Net worth is the sum total of your
    _____, _____ and
    investments and can be positive or negative, depending
    on how much you own or how much you owe.

14. What is the formula for determining your net worth?

15. Yes or No: I frequently see other people grab an
    opportunity that I failed to identify.

16. Yes or No: I make my own luck.

17. True or False: No matter how bad things look, I never
    give up.

18. Yes or No: I have been told that I lead people very well.

19. True or False: I will succeed if I am in the right place at the right time; I may not succeed if I miss that one opportunity.

20. Yes or No: I am nervous speaking in front of large groups.

21. Yes or No: A budget is an essential tool for managing money.

22. Yes or No: I tend to make purchases on impulse.

23. _____ is the way to grow the money that I don't use to meet my daily needs.

24. ___% is the ideal amount to begin saving from my income.

25. Yes or No: I have a vision of where I would like to be in five years and ten years.

Answers

Now check your answers against the answers we have provided below. See what your score has to say about you.

1. What are most of our spending patterns when teens and adults based upon? **Childhood experiences with money**

2. "I think, therefore I am" is a simple rule to increase what?
   Your earning potential

3. When passion is combined with action and **perseverance**, true wealth can be created.

4. Events or circumstances that operate for or against an individual – that are not a direct result of their own efforts - are called what?
   Luck

5. The law of tithing suggests that what percentage of your net income should be given away? **10%**

6. What one factor can keep a person motivated about their work? **Passion or Purpose**

7. True or False: Wealthy people avoid negativity. **True**

8. True or False: People who will become wealthy behave as if they are already wealthy. They associate with wealthy people and learn from them. **True**

9. Yes or No: Do you feel it is important to make a mark in the life? **Yes**

10. Yes or No: Are you prepared to take risks in life? **Yes**

11. Yes or No: Do you find decision-making difficult? **No**

12. Yes or No: I dislike negotiating over prices or other aspects of business. **No**

13. Net worth is the sum total of your **assets, savings** and investments and can be positive or negative, depending on how much you own or how much you owe.

14. What is the formula for determining your net worth? **Assets minus Liabilities**

15. Yes or No: I frequently see other people grab an opportunity that I failed to identify. **No**

16. Yes or No: I make my own luck. **Yes**

17. True or False: No matter how bad things look, I never give up. **True**

18. Yes or No: I have been told that I lead people very well. **Yes**

19. True or False: I will succeed if I am in the right place at the right time but I may not succeed if I miss that one opportunity. **False**

20. Yes or No: I am nervous speaking in front of large groups. **No**

21. Yes or No: A budget is an essential tool for managing money. **Yes**

22. Yes or No: I tend to make purchases on impulse. **No**

23. **Investing or Investments** is the way to grow the money that I don't use to meet my daily needs.

24. 10% is the ideal amount to begin saving from my income.

25. Yes or No: I have a vision of where I would like to be in 5 and 10 years. **Yes**

How to Grade Your ⓔ Potential Scores:

If you got all 25 correct, you are sure to realize your full potential!

If you got 20-24 correct, you are well on your way to success. Study further and with some hard work, you'll become successful.

If you got 15-19 correct, you will be successful if you seriously start to focus on your priorities and adjust your lifestyle to ensure wealth.

If you got 10-14 correct, you must spend more time focusing on learning the skills of money management.

If you got less than 10 correct, you should study the materials again, paying close attention to the tips and techniques used to grow wealth so that you can have a better chance of becoming successful too.

Entrepreneurship and You

Today's generation of teens longs to be successful and rich almost before they are out of the cradle. They have no patience. They have been fed a diet of instant remedies for everything their entire lives. To them, the idea of working for most of their lives in a steady job is laughable. They are much more inclined to believe they can scrimp and save and 'fluke' their way to millionaire status.

This attitude is in sharp contrast to the one most mentors grew up with: One in which people held one job for the majority of their adult lives and looked forward to a retirement supported by their pensions or retirement accounts. The tragedy is that the system is ill-equipped to support the dream. Many people who believed they were doing the wise and sensible thing have found themselves facing scandals and bankruptcies at every turn. Small wonder, then, that today's youth turns up its collective nose at our outmoded ideas and opts for get-rich quick schemes to achieve financial freedom.

The irony is that, because the system we grew up with has virtually bankrupted itself, the subject of money and the pursuit of financial and personal freedom have never been so popular and so respected. It is no longer crass to hunger to be financially free. Nowadays, it is considered proof of clear-headed thinking to be able to create a good life and realize your *ⓔ Potential* at a young age.

While it is safe to say that most young people dream of owning their own businesses and being successful, it isn't everyone whose dreams actually come true. The Money Basket formula has enabled many people to launch new ventures, but they don't always succeed. It takes a unique mindset and a specific set of skills to run your own business successfully once it has been launched. This unique mindset and set of skills belong to an extraordinary type of individual known as the 'entrepreneur'.

On the preceding pages, we have explained that _success_ is much more than a goal or a state of mind. It is also a language that is unlike any other. However, a language is only an effective tool if you understand it and know how it is spoken.

Entrepreneurship is the way people speak the language of success, using it to communicate their ideas and profit from them.

We have created an Entrepreneurship questionnaire to help you recognize your strengths and identify your weaknesses as a means to help you become a true entrepreneur.

With your mentor reading out the questions that follow, listen closely. Answer each one with a 'Yes' or a 'No'.

1. When you find yourself having to make tough decisions, do you trust your instincts or do you look to others to make the choices for you?

2. Do you act on your decisions or second-guess yourself?

3. If you make a mistake, do you throw in the towel?

4. Do you see 'failure' as an opportunity to learn?

5. Do you see problems as puzzles waiting to be solved?

6. Do you see challenge as an opportunity to grow?

7. Does change excite you?

8. Do you expect to win?

9. Do you see yourself as a can-do person who rises to a challenge?

10. Do you see problems or opportunities in the obstacles you find blocking your path?

11. Do you welcome the chance to share the burden and reap the rewards that come with being part of a strong team?

12. Are you a 'one person show' who finds it hard to take orders from others?

13. Do you prefer to work alone?

14. Do you need to make a difference?

15. Do you set goals that challenge you?

16. Do you look for opportunities to learn and grow?

17. Does the idea of taking a calculated risk excite you?

18. Are you willing to dedicate yourself to achieve your goal?

19. Are you willing to listen and accept new ideas?

20. Can you accept criticism easily?

21. Can you change?

22. Do you put your best foot forward?

23. Does your attitude inspire others?

24. Do people gravitate toward you?

25. Do they like your ideas and look to you for answers?

26. Do you think twice and act once?

27. Do you apply careful consideration or trust to luck?

28. Are you a bargain hunter?

29. Are you a natural born sales person?

30. Do you enjoy the process?

31. Would you rather just get it done?

32. Do you see opportunity in all things?

33. Are you full of ideas to make money?

34. Do you see deal-making as the best part of business?

35. Do you look after your health?

36. Do you eat right, exercise and get plenty of rest?

37. Do you take on challenges to keep your mind alert?

38. Do you have unlimited reserves of energy and enthusiasm?

39. Do you have a plan for your future?

40. Do you see yourself in control?

41. Do you keep going?

42. Do you let setbacks stand in your way?

43. Do you think people make their own luck?

44. Is success a function of working smart?

45. Do you thrive on the challenge that growth and change can bring to your life?

46. Are you willing to settle for less than the best?

47. Do you like to keep track of the details?

48. Do you prefer to focus on the big picture and let the details take care of themselves?

49. Do you like to do everything yourself to be sure it's right?

50. Do you prefer to delegate the work and focus on growing the business instead?

When you have completed the Entrepreneurship questionnaire above, go back and examine the answers and discuss with your mentor what you need to do to enhance your financial future and achieve ultimate success.

Thomas Edison was a brilliant inventor with a clever wit. He said that genius was one-part inspiration and ninety-nine parts perspiration.

What he meant by that statement was that to succeed at anything, you have to be prepared to work for it. Working for it means rolling up your sleeves and doing the physical tasks, sure. But it also means working hard to change your old mindset into one of Wealth and Success thinking, and into beliefs that support your own potential to succeed at anything you undertake.

Before you invest your money in launching your own business, be sure that you have invested the time it takes to prepare yourself – from the inside out – to launch any new venture.

Don't make the mistake of thinking a product or a service will be a big success because _you_ like it. Why? You are not your customer. You aren't going to be the one buying it. You need to do the research about the demand for and attractiveness of your business product. Double-check the facts; get second and third opinions from as many experts as you can; talk to lots of people before you take your money out of the bank.

You can have a fabulous future if you think carefully, plan wisely, commit yourself to the cause and give it all you've got!

Making It All Work For You

You began with the talents and skills and interests that God gave you. You now have the tools to create the abundance model that will bring you wealth, success and happiness.

1.a.　As a mentor, do you want to be more successful?

If your answer is 'Yes', you need to use this book as a daily reference guide. You need to share it with your loved ones so they understand. You need to believe in yourself and your dreams and go for it.

1.b.　*Why?* Why do you want to be more successful?

2.a.　As a teen, do you want to make it big while you're still young?

If your answer is 'Yes', you need to listen to your mentor. You need to learn the lessons and apply the formulas outlined in this book. You need to be willing to step outside your comfort zone and ignore the anger and fear you will sense from many of your peers (anger that you are moving beyond what they feel they can do; fear that you'll drag them into your folly!).

2.b.　*Why?* Why do you want to make it big right now?

3.a.   As a team, do you want to find the path to wealth
       and make your dreams come true?

       If your answer is 'Yes', the tools are in your hand. It is
       up to you to work together to support each other
       and make it work for you.

3.b.   *Why?* Why do you seek wealth? Why do you need
       your dreams to come true?

I put you on the spot by asking '*Why*?', didn't I?

It is far too easy to pay lip service to wealth, success and
happiness... and then to do nothing to create it.

When you ask yourself for the *reasons* you want these
things, you dive more deeply into your real motivation.
When you are really motivated is when you commit to a
plan to succeed in materializing your dreams, your wealth
and your success.

It's Not Them; It's Not Their Life

In most cultures, there are some traditions and expectations that are not always discussed out loud, but that *everyone "knows" about.* What a youngster does with his adult life is one of those topics! It is one of the biggest root causes of the so-called "generation gap." It is only worse when peer pressure turns up the heat.

- Your parents may want you to be the family's 3rd generation medical doctor, but you are totally motivated by creating fine art.
- Your three best friends may be really into writing and selling Horror Romance Fiction as e-books and trying to pull you in with them, while you are more drawn to designing and making furniture.
- Your family elders may not understand what a 'mobile app' is and so don't get why you devote yourself to creating them.

Ask, answer and really *know* the reasons for you. Not for your parents or friends – but for you. Outside push and outside cajoling will never work like your own internal motivation to create your success.

Working toward satisfying those deeper motivations is what will keep you going.

PART SIX:

Carly's Diary

Carly's Diary

Hi, Everyone! I'm so excited that you're finally here! I hope you enjoyed learning about the Savings Baskets and that the ⓔ Potential and Entrepreneur tests opened your eyes to some cool new ideas!

The pages that follow are taken from my Diary. Because it isn't often that you get to hear how a teen feels about the things that parents want, my Mom and I thought it would be a good idea if you got to see what I was thinking as I began my own journey as a Wealthy Teen.

Okay, I'm going to let you get to it. Bye for now!

Dear Diary,

Today's D-Day. I should call it A-day, because this is when I get my allowance of $10. It may not sound like much, but every little bit helps to grow my savings Basket, my fun Basket, my investment Basket, my car Basket...

On my dressing table I have these 5 big glass jars that I got at the Dollar store. I wanted to be able to see the money adding up.

In each of them, I divide whatever money I get, no matter how little or how much it is. Even if I find a dollar on the ground, I make the change and divide it up. Doing that puts me in control and it is a great feeling to watch my money grow.

This is how I divide it:

10%	10%	10%	20%	50%
Savings	Fun	Charity	Investments	Essentials

I start with SAVINGS because I want to pay myself first. Then I pay for my FUN. After that, I give something to the Charity of my Choice. I want to have a car by the time I'm 16, so for me the Investments jar is really my Car Basket. And finally, there are things that I have to do and have. Those are my Essentials.

As I put everything in, I keep a written record that I add up as I go along. It helps me know at a glance how much I have in each account and where the money came from.

My mom helped me open an account at the bank so I can transfer my long-term investment money into a savings account at the bank. When a great opportunity comes up, I'll invest my money and let it go to work earning interest for me.
Right now, I'm getting interest on it from 2.4% or more. If I want, my mentor can help me invest in a mutual fund or stocks at a later stage and help get me a higher return on my money!

Doing all the steps to manage my money and plan for my future is a lot like studying to become something – I haven't decided what I'm going to be yet: maybe a famous photographer, or a fashion designer. In the meantime, I'm doing all this money management stuff so my money can become big and strong!

Dear Diary,

Yesterday I made a Brownie cake for a friend's birthday party and got paid $12. The ingredients cost $4, so that was a clear profit of $8: Not bad for half an hour's work. I was thinking of doing it as a business, but I thought about it a little longer and realized that I'd be up to my elbows in Baskets and flour, making cakes all day long and that's just wrong! I want my money to work hard, not me!

Okay. I've just looked at my numbers and my current balance shows totally cool figures. And you know something else? I've also noticed that if I follow my Wealthy Teen Basket Plan, doing the 10%/10%/10%/10%/50% breakdown, I always get more money. If I miss it even once and just spend the money I get, I end up with less. I am like, totally addicted to this plan. Good thing it's a very healthy, wealthy addiction!

Carly's POA (Plan of Action)

Diary, I wanted to write down a few things to remember:

<u>Mission</u>: Get a head start to success.

<u>Thoughts</u>:
Is there more to money than just money?

Do I want to be really smart and have the IQ of a genius or do I want to be someone with a lot of cool ideas about making money and enjoying my wealth?

<u>Important</u>: Anyone can make money to be successful.

<u>Things to do:</u>
Talk about it
Read about it
Write about it
Take it seriously
Do my accounts every day
Become responsible for my future.
Don't plan to depend on <u>anyone</u>
Create money (how)
<u>Asset</u> = money in
<u>Liability</u> = money out (or still owed to someone)

Learning is my formula to success!

Dear Diary,

I so desperately wanted to buy a Tamagotchi - it's a real craving. But somehow I held on for a week and then suddenly the craving passed and I didn't want the Tamagotchi anymore. Now I'd rather have an mp3 player...

The point is, I get influenced really easily, but because I know I get influenced I try to hold on to see if I want something because I really want it or if I want it because I think I want it. Sounds really confusing, but I know what I mean by that...

I have decided to tell myself that whenever I desperately want something I can have it ... after a week!

So far it works well. Is it because I gave myself permission to buy it and that's why I no longer want it? Very confusing. Will need to have a big discussion later with my mentor.

Money Saving Tips

I am writing down a few money-saving tips, because when I need them I don't remember them. I'll keep adding more as I need to.

1. *Drink 3 glasses of water before going out (healthy for you and then you don't need to buy POP. If you can, carry water).*

2. Carry your own juice and if it's not too uncool, a snack (granola bar, fruit, sandwich ... whatever)
3. DON'T go shopping on an empty stomach! Very, very important.
4. Eat on time so you don't get sugar lows.
5. Stick to healthy foods.
6. Carry fruit with you.
7. Keep a record of all your expenses. (idea: should I design small notepads and sell them? I could call them + or -).
8. Don't get carried away at sales.
9. Be a leader, not a follower.
10. Don't do what everyone else is doing just because they're doing it.
11. Keep some money aside for impulse buying (like my fun bank), so I don't fall off the wagon.
12. When I want something big, instead of thinking 'I can't afford it' or 'I wish I could,' think of ways to make it possible. (Haven't tried it yet, but will soon).
13. Try to combine errands and save time. Make a map.
14. Don't follow fashion blindly.
15. Buy clothes that will last a bit, not the 'Flavor of the Day'.
16. Watch movies on DVD/video instead of always going out.
17. Set a weekly budget – this to spend, this for food, etc.
18. Do odd jobs for extra money.
19. Is there any way to make the money (I already have) grow?
20. Invent my own money tree?
21. Plan your Days and your life.

22. Be time savvy. This day will never come back ... nor this month ... nor this year.
23. Don't be a cheapskate, but be realistic.
24. Think positive.
25. Think rich!

Dear Diary,

A friend of mine called to ask me to let her know if I knew anyone who was selling a bike. I didn't know then, but I called her today to tell her my neighbor was selling a bike and she came and got it. Both of them are happy.

Is there an idea here?

Garage sale

How to get A to meet B

How about a Garage Sale online?

Dear Diary,

It has been a few days. I've been thinking about the garage sale thingy and I searched online too, but found nothing great. So I have been thinking ... and sort of discussed my idea with mom.

Here is the breakdown of expenses (if I want to hold a garage sale online):

Website set-up cost: $200 dollars (for the design too). Monthly Fee: $10 a month

Questions I have to discuss with mom and get answers to:

How will I advertise?
How will I make money?

Note to myself:
I am so excited! If it works, it will be my very own system to make money. I am putting my money to work and learning about Mom's "entrepreneurship" idea. (Gee, that's a mouthful. If I could change it, I'd call it something cool, like 'Biz Whiz'. At least I can say AND spell that! Oh well. What counts isn't what you call it but how it works, right?)

Note to myself:
Could I be a Biz Whiz in the making? Research great entrepreneurs and see what makes them great. Should be interesting.

Dear Diary,

Mom likes my idea of the garage sale and we are working on the other points, like how to make money from it, how to advertise ...so many things. Sometimes, I get really worried, but at other times I am so excited. Mom says it's a bit like learning to fly (I think she means learning anything new). It's really scary, and then suddenly you know how to do it.

Anyway, I am having fun and it's great to learn all this. It's like real life ... not playing.

Dear Diary,

Here are some of the qualities great entrepreneurs have in common.

Creative
Organized
Passionate
Practical
Enterprising
Dedicated
Unafraid

Dear Diary,

I had a sort of a fight with my best friend. She only wants to hang out at the mall, but I am so busy with my stuff now that I really don't want to go. When I tried to explain to her, she called me money-minded. That's so unfair. She's always wishing she had money to buy stuff and always complaining that she never gets to do anything new ... Why are things always so difficult?

Anyway, here is where I have reached.

The designing for the garage sale website is underway. I have the name I want. And I am going to advertise through email (I'll email my friends and ask them to tell all their friends) and then let's see.

My mom thinks it will be a real learning experience for me.

Dear Diary,

Everything is ready to roll. I paid for everything out of my own money from my Investment Basket.

Let's see how it goes. I am soooo excited and also so worried! What if I fall flat on my face? Guess I'll just have to get back up and try again.

Dear Diary,

Guess what? My best friend wants to know how I got such a cool site together and how I paid for it. She doesn't want to be broke anymore. So I am going to give her my Plan of Action.

And guess what, I made my first money today: $5! My money worked for me, not the other way around!!!!!

Yippee! I am on the path to success.

P.S. My friend's not angry with me anymore.

Carly's POA [Plan of Action]

Here's what I did when I got started. I am going to pass it on to my friends who want to learn too (they think I'm a genius, but the real thing is managing my money and not letting it manage me).

Anyway here goes. The **Plan of Action** starts after you have read the book, 'The Wealthy Teen'.

Day 1: Start thinking about money. What does it mean to you? Look at the 5 things you filled out in chapter 2 in "TWT".
Keep a daily diary with your thoughts and ideas and questions.

Day 2-5: Think about what you want in life: Your hopes and dreams. Do you want to just get along? Do you want to be comfortable or be rich?

Day 6-10: Analyze your expenses. Then analyze them again. There's lots of stuff you don't really need, even though you think you do.

Day 11-14: List everything you spend money on. Be aware of where your money is going and what you are spending. (Check out the Expense/Income daily sheet – after this section).

Day 15: Go to the library and pick up (or place a hold for) books on money and investing.

Day 16: Have your mom/dad/guardian subscribe to good financial magazines like Money Sense *or the* Wall Street Journal *and try to read them.*

Day 17: Talk to your friends about it. Start a Wealthy Teen Club. Think of ways to make money as a group. Give each person a separate task.

Day 18-20: Analyze how your thinking has changed since you read this book.

Day 21-25: Make up your Wealthy Teen plan and stick to it. Get five piggy banks and label them, fun, saving, charity, investment and essentials. Put the money in like this:

10% in savings   10% in fun   10% in charity
20% in long-term savings for investment   50% for essentials

Sounds complicated, but once you have control over money, it will fly to you (Like a bee to honey! Corny but true).

Day 26-28: Discuss your goals with your family so they will be able to support your ideas and you can all work together.

Day 30: Read over your diary entries and compare the way you think and feel now to the way you did a month ago. Read the answers you gave when you read 'The Wealthy Teen' the first time and see how far you have come.

Daily: Keep daily financial records.
Weekly: Review your progress and try to keep track about how you are progressing mentally.

Read the book as often as you need it and keep up with your daily diary entries. One day you'll want to look back when you're wealthy and see how you did it!

BEFORE WE SAY GOOD-BYE

Carly and I wanted to take a minute to say a few last words before we sent *The Wealthy Teen* off to the publisher.

We began writing this book to help others find the path to wealth and success as a team just as we had, but we discovered something else was happening as we wrote.

That's right! What my Mom and I learned was how totally cool it was to think and act like two equals sharing a goal!

Carly is so right. I don't think any parent entirely recognizes that their children are completely separate entities with creative ideas and minds of their own, until they start working with them as equals in search of a common goal.

Even though I've been a human resources professional for many years and work as a consultant and coach now, it hadn't dawned on me that my daughter was capable of having such mature insights and clever ideas... until they appeared fully formed on the pages as she wrote.

This brought home to me with even more emphasis the incredible power you have when you work as a team, mentor and teen, to realize your dreams. I can't urge you strongly enough to give it a try.

Carly:

Me too! I always knew my Mom was smart. What I didn't know until now was how much fun she was to just hang out with and talk about all the things I've never told anyone before. Writing The Wealthy Teen *with her has been the best thing that's happened to me... so far!*

Good luck on your journey.

Best Wishes and Best Success on your journey to creating your ⓔ *Potential!*

If you want to reach out to us – please go to:

www.thewealthyteen.com

Lorna and Carly

www.ingramcontent.com/pod-product-compliance
Lightning Source LLC
LaVergne TN
LVHW051459080426
835509LV00017B/1824